PAGE-TURNER

*Your Path to Writing a Novel That
Publishers Want and Readers Buy*

BARBARA KYLE

Page-Turner

ISBN 978-0-9877206-5-8 (print)
ISBN 978-0-9877206-6-5 (eBook)

Also by Barbara Kyle

The Traitor's Daughter
The Queen's Exiles
Blood Between Queens
The Queen's Gamble
The Queen's Captive
The King's Daughter
The Queen's Lady
Entrapped
The Experiment

PRAISE FOR BARBARA KYLE'S
PAGE-TURNER

"Kyle knows her stuff. She's one of the rare authors who can break down both the art and the craft of writing in a way that is entertaining and easy to understand."

—#1 NEW YORK TIMES BESTSELLING AUTHOR
KELLEY ARMSTRONG

"Barbara Kyle is a wonderful writing teacher, and she brings her teaching style to life in this page-turner."

—LEE GOWAN, PROGRAM DIRECTOR, CREATIVE WRITING,
UNIVERSITY OF TORONTO SCHOOL OF CONTINUING STUDIES

"Barbara Kyle has keen novelistic instincts and in Page-Turner *she brings alive almost every tough issue a writer of fiction must confront. She does this with impeccably chosen and most helpful examples drawn from her own fine writing and from a wide range of classics and bestsellers. And* Page-Turner *is friendly and fun to read."*

—ALBERT ZUCKERMAN, FOUNDER OF
WRITERS HOUSE LITERARY AGENCY

PRAISE FOR BARBARA KYLE'S STORY COACHING

"Barbara Kyle's evaluation was a game changer for me. I received advice and suggestions that vastly improved my manuscript's clarity and vision. Working with Barbara is like having a secret weapon in your writing arsenal."
—NANCY RAVEN SMITH, AUTHOR OF *Land Sharks*

"Barbara Kyle is a master storyteller, and she's especially gifted at helping writers see what's still missing in their work."
—MARY ANN MCGUIGAN, AUTHOR OF *Crossing Into Brooklyn*

"Barbara quickly identified the weaknesses in my story and helped me strategize how to transform them into strengths. I am grateful for the positive encouragement she provided."
—JAKE CALDERA, AUTHOR OF *The Elephant on Fire*

"Barbara played an essential part in my writing journey."
—ROSANNA BATTIGELLI, AUTHOR OF *La Brigantessa*

"Barbara is the single best writing teacher I have ever had."
—TOM TAYLOR, AUTHOR OF *Brock's Assassin*

"I took Barbara Kyle's excellent Master Class when I was stuck with my first novel. Those two great days were a turning point. I recently

finished my fourth book and Barbara's wise words about plot, dialogue, voice – and most of all character – constantly guide my way."

 —ROBERT ROTENBERG, AUTHOR OF *Stray Bullets*

"Barbara's evaluation delivered thorough, detailed feedback that taught me a lot about the craft. She told me exactly what she (and agents and publishers) seek, and gave me specific comments about what did and did not work in my story, and why."

 —MATT PHILLIPS

"I took Barbara's advice and loved the result."

 —MARISSA CAMPBELL, AUTHOR OF *Avelynn*

"I had the good fortune to attend several of Barbara Kyle's workshops. They provided a wealth of knowledge on all aspects of writing and publishing, and valuable feedback on my own writing… her insightful evaluation encouraged me to complete the novel."

 —*M.G. FIELD*, AUTHOR OF *Incarceration*

"Barbara Kyle enlightened me how to mend my wayward chapters and knock my plot into a compelling story. Few can do what she has: taking a good amateur writer to the elite few of a top New York agent."

 —RICO PROVASOLI, AUTHOR OF *Please Don't Tell My Guru*

"I learned more from Barbara Kyle in a half-hour than I have in countless workshops and books. A riveting, energetic, and positive experience."

 —TRISH KERR, TORONTO WRITERS & EDITORS NETWORK

"An exciting tale of the intrigue and political manoeuvring in the Tudor court."
 —Booklist on *The Queen's Captive*

"Action-packed adventure that expertly blends fiction with history ... a pulsating story of valor and greed, love and passion, and the tremendous cost of loyalty."
 —Publishers Weekly blog on *The Queen's Gamble*

"Riveting, heady, glorious, inspired."
 —Susan Wiggs on *The Queen's Lady*

"A classic historical novel – sweeping, gritty and realistic."
 —Historical Novel Society on *The Queen's Lady*

"Kyle creates a taut thriller where family loyalty and patriotism collide ... keeps readers hooked."
 – RT Book Reviews on *The Traitor's Daughter*

"Riveting, adventurous ... superb!"
 —Historical Novel Society on *The Queen's Gamble*

"Many jolts and twists and turns that will leave no one unsatisfied."
 —Giles Blunt on *Entrapped*

"A haunting thriller ... Kyle keeps the cinematic action scenes and nail-biting suspense rolling throughout."
 —Publishers Weekly on *The Experiment*

An Invitation

We are always learning—established authors and emerging writers alike —engaged in a life-long exploration of our fascinating craft. You've purchased *Page-Turner*, a step along this exploration trail.

To help you further, I invite you to subscribe to my Newsletter for Writers. You'll get information about upcoming workshops, master classes, online courses, and webinars, plus contests, giveaways, and special discounts. Sign up with one click on my website: www.BarbaraKyle.com.

I look forward to getting to know you better as you move forward on the path toward published success.

All my best,

Barbara Kyle

bkyle@barbarakyle.com
www.BarbaraKyle.com

Contents

CHAPTER 1

ANATOMY OF A PAGE-TURNER

While my husband lay sleeping, I slipped out of bed and down the hall. I moved quietly, but my brain was shouting the idea that had woken me. I reached my office and stood at my desk, too keyed-up to sit, as I scrawled these four words: "Ralph Pepperton must die."

Don't worry, that impulsive moment did not lead me to commit a murder. Rather, it led to a birth: the birth of a book. To be more accurate, it jolted life into a story. It was the first novel I had attempted, and I'd been struggling with it, a lifeless, tangled sprawl of vignettes, until that pre-dawn jolt of inspiration. Ralph's death would devastate my heroine, spurring her to take action that would create a conflict to propel the narrative. Ralph Pepperton saved my book.

You've had the same kind of stirring experience—I know you have. An idea bursts upon you, blazing the way to move your story forward. It's one of the joys of being a writer. As for me, I'm forever grateful to Ralph for sacrificing his life all those years ago. His death gave birth to my writing career. My publisher sold over 75,000 copies of that novel, *The Queen's Lady*, and it became the first in a seven-book series, The Thornleigh Saga.

Ralph's was just the first death. Since then, in my subsequent historical novels and contemporary thrillers, I've cut short the lives of over a dozen very nasty people who deserved it, scores of poor souls who didn't, and about a thousand innocent bystanders. I've hanged them, poisoned them, burned them at the stake, electrified them, slit their throats, shot them, and beheaded them. Not, of course, in that order.

But deaths are easy. (As the actor Edmund Gwen is reported to have said on his deathbed, "Dying is easy. Comedy is hard.") It is death's *opposite* that quickens a writer's pulse. Creation. Nothing compares to the thrill of creating characters, and making their lives so real that readers wish the story wouldn't end.

The challenge for the emerging writer is how to achieve that. How does one fashion such a story? A page-turner. The fact that you're reading these pages shows you're serious about learning the answer.

This book has one purpose: to give you the practical, in-depth information you need to write a richly engaging story that can compete in today's competitive publishing marketplace. I'll be your mentor to guide you, but make no mistake, you are the hero of this story. It's *your* book we want to bring to the world.

The word "hero" in the classic, literary sense means someone who is on a quest, a challenging one, and on the way learns something profound. And the word "mentor" in the classic, literary sense means someone who prepares the hero to embark on that quest. Your desire to perfect your craft as a writer is a meaningful quest. In fact, I consider it a noble calling, because humanity lives by its stories. In his book *The Writer's Journey* Christopher Vogler outlines twelve steps of a hero's journey, the final one being "Return With the Elixir." The hero brings something back from the adventure—an "elixir" either literal or metaphoric—that heals the tribe, or mends the marriage, or saves the world. Dorothy in *The Wizard of Oz* brings back the knowledge that "There's no place like home." Your book can be an "elixir" because you have something to say to the world. But only by perfecting your craft can you say it in a way that will reach a wide readership.

In my career as an internationally published author I've faced every challenge you're facing now. So I speak to you as writer to writer. Having worked in this business for years, I know what agents and publishers are looking for, what they want—and don't want.

What they always want, whatever the book's genre or its target audience, is a page-turner. A book that leaves readers saying, "I couldn't put it down!"

Your most important step toward success is to take your writing seriously. I don't mean take yourself seriously, none of us should do that; we're all fools. I mean that when you sit down to write you do it with serious intent, no half-hearted dabbling.

I've mentored hundreds of emerging writers in my role as an instructor of university courses, in workshops at writers' conferences, and through my story coaching via manuscript evaluations, and I've found that the way writers respond to my critiques often indicates whether they're committed to succeeding. Many feel energized by a new clarity of vision. (As one put it, "a light bulb moment.") One such writer sent me a Young Adult novel that was superbly written and very moving but lacked focus, which drained its power. I pointed out how she could tighten the central conflict and refocus the sub-plot. She did so with verve, and her rewritten manuscript attracted a top New York literary agent who now represents her.

To another writer I recommended that his very long manuscript be radically trimmed to liberate the fine adventure story buried beneath a smother of overgrown description. When I identified the specific deadwood that could be cut back, he understood immediately and was eager to embark on the necessary slash-and-burn mission.

And, I fondly recall a writer at one of my workshops who read aloud her exercise, a summary of events in the all-important scene introducing her story's protagonist. She read it to the group, and then, in the nervous silence that followed, looked at me and said, "It's boring, isn't it?" That brought laughter from us all, including her, and I applaud that writer for being so open to change. I pointed out *why* the scene was boring—that the protagonist was passive, just idly observing others—and suggested, as a solution, that she introduce the character engaged in an action with something at stake. She was delighted.

Writers like these are a joy to work with. Their open-minded attitude gives them the best chance of succeeding.

Then there are others. Some are so defensive about their work they're deaf to suggestions for improving it. Some consider writing as merely a take-it-or-leave-it hobby, or as therapy. Some have the talent to produce a promising first draft but balk at the work necessary for a second and third draft. These positions drastically reduce their chances of getting published. The creation of a compelling and marketable book has to fully engage one's energy, mind, and heart. Every serious writer is trying to be a great writer.

Not that success is the *only* reward to writing. Kurt Vonnegut put it quite beautifully when he said, "Practicing an art, no matter how well or badly, is a way to make your soul grow, for heaven's sake. Sing in the shower. Dance to the radio. Tell stories. Write a poem to a friend, even a lousy poem. Do it as well as you possibly can. You will get an enormous reward. You will have created something."

Lovely advice. And true.

But I want more for you. I want your manuscript to be seen beyond a handful of friends and family. I want you to succeed as a writer in the global marketplace. I want you to sign with that agent, and land that publishing deal, and have your book bought by a wide audience of thrilled readers. That requires serious work.

Our culture has an interesting expression: "work of art." There's a tension between those two nouns, "work" and "art." We tend to revere art, elevating it to a mythical level. Critics cultivate the image of the artist touched by genius, while work is denigrated, as though no real artist wrestles with something so mundane; as though writing shouldn't be work at all if a writer has "talent." Nonsense. Nothing could be further from the truth. I suggest that we let the critics and other non-writers obsess about art. We writers will concern ourselves with the work. My recommendation is this: embrace the work.

I sometimes wish we had another word for it. "Work" connotes something tedious, dismal, endless. The cliché images are bleak. Nose to the grindstone, punching a clock, slaves. But the work of writing isn't anything like that. There's no backbreaking labor, no tyrannical boss, and because the energy source is your imagination, there's no restriction on the content you produce. Writing can be a profound pleasure.

However, because of this very freedom, the work of writing requires concentration, and focus, and will. I like the advice of author Wayson Choy: "There's only one secret to writing: A/C—ass on chair." You sit down and write, then re-write, then re-write. There is no other way to master the craft.

I think it's helpful to focus on a different word—not "work" but "process," as in "It's a process." One theme of the enchanting film *Shakespeare in Love* is the magic of the theater. Screenwriters Tom Stoppard and Marc Norman have the theater owner reassure his anxious investor about the quixotic process of creating a show. In rehearsals, he says, it might seem like the play will never come together, but in the end it always does. "It's a mystery," he adds with a happy shrug.

That's true, in part, about writing a novel too. Your individual nature—your world view, your sensibilities shaped by your unique experiences—will direct much of what you write and how you write, and that aspect of the process will always remain something of a mystery. There's little you can do about your own nature, and that's fine; it will color your writing with your voice, as it should. But, with all due respect, the process is not about you; it's about creating an invisible interface between your story's characters and the reader. That's what you *do* have control over, and that's *not* a mystery. All the basics of the writer's craft can be learned and perfected, in courses, in workshops, in interaction with mentors and editors, and from books like this one. So remember our mantra: embrace the work.

There are no rules in writing. Every rule that's ever been proclaimed has been broken by some writer, somewhere, to good effect. When I began writing years ago I had a mentor who said, "There's only one rule in writing: thou shalt not bore." Good advice.

So, okay, apart from that one, there are no rules. But there are principles that have shaped the art of storytelling for centuries, and the wise writer studies them. A rule says: do this. A principle says: this works, and it has worked through all of remembered time. Those timeless principles of storytelling form the core of this book. They are encapsulated in what I call the Three "A"s:

ACTORS

People. A book's characters. They are the lifeblood of your story. People are what readers come to a book for, and why they stay. Long after a book's plot intricacies and carefully sculpted sentences have become a blur in the reader's memory, what lingers is the impact of the characters. Vibrant, unique characters live on for years, even—like Ebenezer Scrooge—for centuries.

ARCHITECTURE

Story structure. The backbone of your book. You likely have a good instinct for this already, but that will take you only half the way. When instinct falls short and talent gets stuck, an understanding of story structure gets you moving again. This knowledge is essential, yet often under-appreciated by emerging writers. The cleverest wordsmith and most gifted creator of characters cannot bring these riches to a wide audience unless they are delivered in the "story" form the human mind is hard-wired to receive.

ADORNMENT

Style. The actual words you write. I use the somewhat dismissive term "adornment" to convey the vital truth that of the Three "A"s, style is the least crucial. Don't misunderstand—word choice is very important. Tinted by evocative imagery, it can even be sublime. But a deeply engaging story with vibrant characters will live for a reader even if the prose is unadorned. The reverse is not true: exquisite prose cannot carry a stagnant story about dull people.

So what, exactly, constitutes a page-turner? What is the mysterious literary essence that hooks a reader? What holds them so hard, they simply must keep reading, often long into the night? To emerging writers who want to break in, and published authors who want to produce a breakout book, I offer a one-word answer. Emotion.

Sounds simplistic? After all, I've just gone on about the hard work you must do to perfect the many complex facets of our craft, to create evocative characters, hone your story structure, and chisel finely sculpted sentences. But structure and style are not ends in themselves. They are merely tools to produce the result we want: an emotional experience for the reader.

It's why children gleefully cry, "Read it again!" It's why, after over four hundred years, Shakespeare's characters continue to enthrall us, because they tap into a profound emotional wellspring. When characters in a story move your readers to pity, or laughter, or loathing, or dread, or just the simple warmth of human fellow-feeling, *that's* what makes them keep turning pages. They crave to know: what's going to happen to these people? They *care*. The fine details of craft drift past the reader like mist unless the hand of emotion reaches out to snag them and hold them.

Raymond Chandler, a founder of the noir mystery genre in the 1940s, knew this. Here was a writer famous for his action stories—as he put it, stories that were "tough and fast and full of mayhem and murder"—yet he said: "Readers just thought that they cared about nothing but the action; but really although they didn't know it, they cared very little about the action. The thing they really cared about, and that I care about, was the creation of emotion."

The wise writer uses this knowledge. When I mentor writers, I sometimes use the word "manipulate." Effective writing means you're manipulating your reader. It's not a trick. It's anything but shallow. It is, instead, a bonding with humanity's deepest consciousness. What moves us, imprints us. The evoking of emotion is what turns the writer's craft into art.

You've now set out on a journey toward success as a writer. Author Herman Wouk calls it "the long, lonely, stony uphill way of the novel," but I know it's the path you want to be on, or you wouldn't be reading this book. And you'll have me as your guide so you won't get lost in the woods, or lured by enticing sidetracks—the bedazzlement of style, and the giddy false freedom of writing by the seat of your pants, with no plan—that can lead to dead ends.

The poet Robert Frost said "The woods are lovely, dark and deep" but adds the reminder that you "have promises to keep, and miles to go" before you sleep. The most important promise is the one you made to yourself: to write your novel and get it published. This book will help you through the woods. Follow its guideposts. Each chapter contains a cache of information about craft that you'll need on the journey. At the end are pointers on orienting yourself for the last leg, the rocky terrain of the publishing industry.

I know you're ready to stride ahead. How do I know? Because you're reaching out to turn this page.

So turn the page. Grow as a writer. Dare to succeed.

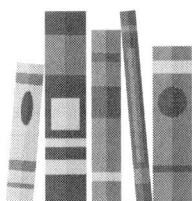

PART I

PEOPLE

CHAPTER 2

INVENTING LIVES

"You take people, you put them on a journey, you give them peril, you find out who they really are."

JOSS WHEDON

Stories are about people.

That seems obvious, doesn't it? Yet new writers often get so carried away constructing elaborate, convoluted plots, or, more commonly, get so engrossed in style—so obsessed with word choice—they forget this simple, essential focus. Stories are about people.

Long after a book's clever plot twists have been forgotten and the author's carefully sculpted prose has become a blur, what lingers in a reader's mind is the impression of the characters. Vibrant, unique characters can live on for decades, sometimes for centuries.

Robinson Crusoe. Moll Flanders. Elizabeth Bennett. Victor Frankenstein. Oliver Twist. Cathy and Heathcliffe. Anna Karenina. Jane Eyre. Ebenezer Scrooge. Sherlock Holmes. Huckleberry Finn. Jeeves. Scarlett O'Hara. Atticus Finch. Lolita. Jay Gatsby. Mary Poppins. Holden Caulfield. 'The Godfather' Don Corleone. Harry Potter. Katniss Everdeen.

You only have to say their names to conjure up entire, distinct worlds.

The Bond of Intimacy

Forging a deep intimacy with characters is why readers love stories. Perhaps it's because in life we can never know everything about anyone. I've lived with my husband for many years and know him very well, but I can never know *exactly* what he's thinking and feeling, what he's hoping and fearing.

In a novel, though, you *can* know people. Here's what E. M. Forster, the author of *A Passage to India* and *Howard's End*, says in one of his 1927 Cambridge lectures collected in the book *Aspects of the Novel*:

> "We cannot understand each other, except in a rough and ready way; we cannot reveal ourselves, even when we want to; what we call intimacy is only a makeshift; perfect knowledge is an illusion. But in the novel we can know people perfectly...and find here a compensation for their dimness in life. In this direction fiction is truer than history, because it goes beyond the evidence, and each of us knows from his own experience that there is something beyond the evidence."

The "something beyond the evidence" is a person's inner, secret life. Or a character's. Glimpsing that inner life and sensing what drives the character, for good or ill, is the connection readers crave.

CHARACTER CREATES PLOT

Critics will sometimes categorize a novel as either "plot driven" or "character driven." When they say a book is "plot driven" it's their shorthand for saying the story is exciting but the characters are a little thin. For example, a Tom Clancy techno-thriller might be called "plot-driven." When a critic says a story is "character driven" that's shorthand for saying the characters are complex and fascinating but the plot is a little thin. Many literary novels, such as *Saturday* by Ian McEwan or *Olive Kitteridge* by Elizabeth Strout, might be called "character driven."

Shorthand may be necessary for critics, but for writers this binary reduction is a false classification. It's meaningless. Because the simple fact is that *all* stories are character driven.

Plot cannot exist without characters. Characters create plot.

What's at work here is causality. E. M. Forster summed it up thus: "The king died and then the queen died," is just a sequence of events, but "The king died and then the queen died of grief" is a plot. The queen's sorrow caused her death. The characters *caused* the plot.

To illustrate this dynamic further, let's look at two of Shakespeare's best-known characters: Hamlet and Romeo. What do we know about Hamlet's character? He is introspective, analytical, cautious. What do we know about Romeo's character? He's passionate, intrepid, bold.

In Act 1 of *Hamlet*, Hamlet encounters the ghost of his dead father who tells him he was murdered by his own brother, Claudius. This stuns Hamlet, for his Uncle Claudius is now married to Hamlet's mother and is king. The play is about Hamlet longing to take revenge on Claudius but being constantly restrained by his own meditative, analytical character. Now, what if Romeo found himself in that situation? Desperate to avenge his father's death, Romeo, being passionate and impetuous, would kill Claudius in Act I and the story would end—there would be no *Hamlet* plot.

Likewise, by the end of Act I of *Romeo and Juliet* Romeo is so madly in love with Juliet he'll risk everything to be with her, even risk being killed by her family. But if Hamlet found himself in Romeo's Act I situation, he might become so engrossed in pondering the existential nature of love that Juliet, unaware that he adores her, would obediently marry Paris, the man her parents have chosen for her, and the story would end. No *Romeo and Juliet* plot.

So, never forget this. Character creates plot. Period.

THE TOP TWO: PROTAGONIST VS. ANTAGONIST

Let's examine the two most important characters you must create: your story's protagonist and its antagonist.

The protagonist—your central character, the hero or heroine—wants and needs something and takes action to try to achieve it. The antagonist wants and needs something too, but that person's goal lies in opposition to the protagonist's. These counterbalanced characters are at the heart of all fiction. Without an antagonist, your protagonist would go about his or her business and there would be no story. As a writer, you want to make choices about character and plot that highlight the conflict between the protagonist and antagonist.

I once heard an interview with bestselling author John LeCarré and he spoke about this concept of conflict. He said, "The cat sat on the mat—that's not a story. But, the cat sat on the dog's mat—that's the beginning of a story."

Can a story's antagonist be a force of nature, like a volcano or a flood? It can. In a famous example, Ernest Hemmingway's *The Old Man and the Sea* pits the fisherman Santiago against the ocean, a marlin, and sharks. However, in the overwhelming majority of novels the conflict will be between human beings.

CONFLICT IS KEY

Science fiction author Nancy Kress puts the concept succinctly: "Fiction is about stuff that's screwed up." All stories spring from conflict. A character who has no problems, no obstacles to overcome, is a boring character. And they are living in a non-story.

As readers, we love to see characters thrown into crisis, forced to grapple with problems. Why? I don't think it's because we're sadists. Rather, it's because we want to experience the emotional bond with a character who faces a dilemma. It's a way of testing ourselves (while facing no actual risk). We get that intense feeling: What would I do in that situation? That's the reason we read stories. Yet new writers often shy away from depicting their characters' conflict. This only undermines the power of their stories.

Instead, I suggest you embrace all the richness that conflict gifts you as a writer. When I'm planning a book, scene by scene, I focus on what the characters do to try to get what they want and how the results of their actions increase the conflict. I do this so constantly, it's become, for me, a kind of comic mantra: "What could possibly go wrong?" I slyly mutter. But actually I'm dead serious. I recommend that you ask yourself this same question, very soberly, about every step of the story you're developing: "What could possibly go wrong?" Then, make that happen.

Nothing moves forward in a story except through conflict.

Furthermore, conflict under pressure is the only way characters truly reveal themselves.

The compelling novel is built on situations that put increasing pressures on characters, forcing them to face more and more difficult challenges, so that they must make increasingly risky choices, leading them to take actions that eventually reveal their true natures.

Three Tips about Conflict

Tip #1. Conflict does not mean combat.

Don't be intimidated by the word conflict. Conflict isn't about fighting. It just means "problems." What problems does your protagonist—your main character—face in trying to achieve his or her goal?

Here's an example. The film *Raining Stones* by British writer/director Ken Loach is the story of a working-class man in northern England who loves his family and his religion. He's poor, but proud, and he's determined to get his little girl the most beautiful dress for her first Communion. But the dress is very expensive, and that's his problem. In his desperation to raise the money, he tries more and more questionable and even dangerous measures, bringing him into conflict with his family, and friends, and eventually the law. This finally leads him to risk all that he loves and values—his family, and even (as he sees it) his immortal soul—in pursuit of his goal. It's a believable and moving story, without any "combat."

The point is, you need to know the central problem your protagonist is facing so that you can keep your story focused on that and not stumble off onto side-tracks.

Tip #2. Escalate the conflict gradually.

To be believable, characters in a story, just like people in real life, will naturally start by taking the most conservative action possible to get what they want. If they don't—if they instantly leap into taking extreme action—they will come across as unrealistic, maybe even a little crazy, and you'll lose your reader. Therefore, the long middle section of your book (for screenwriters it's Act II) will be composed of a series of events that spring from conflict that escalates *gradually*. That is, events force the protagonist to make choices in an ever-escalating series of risks to try to achieve her desire.

She'll start by taking the most minimal, conservative action that she believes will get her what she wants, but instead of bringing success it only arouses a force of antagonism against her. So, can she try the same minimal effort again? If she does, the unimpressed reader will ask: "Hasn't she learned anything?" No, she must now draw on more capacity in herself to take an action that's more forceful, but still moderate—remember, she's not crazy. But the result is only more obstruction. So, does she try moderate action yet again? Not if you want to keep your reader from closing the book for good. Your protagonist must now finally take some extreme, irrevocable action which produces the story's climax. (See more about the importance of this final, irrevocable action in the section on "The Climax" in Chapter 5.)

By the way, this basic principle of escalating conflict applies to comedy as well as drama. The hilarity comes from the ever more absurd lengths the protagonist goes to in going after what they want.

Tip #3. Use more than one level of conflict.

Your protagonist can be in conflict on three possible levels.

1. Internal: conflict with oneself.
2. External Level 1: conflict in interpersonal relationships such as with family, friends, colleagues.
3. External Level 2: extra-personal conflict with the larger community in the form of institutions, such as the government, the church, the school system, the army— institutions that have power.

The most compelling stories, the stories that move us most deeply and stay with us forever, often involve conflict on all three levels: personal, interpersonal, and extra-personal. That's partly what creates the enduring power of books like *David Copperfield, Frankenstein, A Passage to India, Heart of Darkness, The Age of Innocence, The Grapes of Wrath, Gone With the Wind, To Kill a Mockingbird.*

In contrast with those potent stories, it's instructive to examine the form of "soap opera." People often use the term as a pejorative. Why do we do that? After all, soap operas are highly engrossing stories that are loved by millions of viewers. I think the reason we sense weakness in the soap opera form is that it shows us conflict on only one level: the interpersonal. It does that with great panache, it's soap opera's tremendous pull, because interpersonal relationships are so engaging. But it's also incomplete. Characters in a soap opera hardly ever face internal conflict; there's rarely a crisis of conscience. And they never do battle with the larger community. For example, if a cop enters a storyline in a soap, you can be sure he'll soon be caught up in the highly personal concerns of other characters; the story will *not* be about corruption in the police department. So, there's virtually no conflict with the self, nor with society. It's all one level—momentarily highly engrossing, but ultimately unsatisfying.

Not every story can involve conflict on all these levels, but if you can bring all three into your story, I recommend it. The important point is this: never shy away from catching your characters up in the swirling currents of conflict. It will prove their mettle, and make them reveal their true selves. That's what enthralls readers.

When Is the Villain Not a Villain?

A story is only as strong as its antagonist. That's because it's against this character that the protagonist is measured. It's no achievement for your protagonist to vanquish a weakling or a fool. So, make your antagonist a character who is in some way powerful.

In Shakespeare's *Hamlet*, Claudius is the king, so he has power over a country and all its people, including his stepson Hamlet. Darth Vader of the *Star Wars* films has power over an entire astral empire. Moby Dick has immense physical power. Hannibal Lector in Thomas Harris's novel *The Silence of the Lambs* has the power of terror. Antagonists often use such fear to command and control, as does Annie Wilkes, the kidnapper in Stephen King's *Misery*, and Nurse Ratched in Ken Kesey's *One Flew Over the Cuckoo's Nest*. Those women are powerful foes.

But an antagonist's power does not have to be malevolent. It can be simply the hold that one person has over another in a family, a love affair, or a marriage, as Brick does over Maggie in Tennessee Williams's play *Cat on a Hot Tin Roof*. Or it could be simply two people's competing desires, like Jay Gatsby and his nemesis Tom Buchanan in F. Scott Fitzgerald's *The Great Gatsby*, both men wanting the same woman.

Or, the antagonist might be the overwhelming power of a whole society. In John Steinbeck's *The Grapes of Wrath* the force of antagonism is an unrestrained capitalism that condemns workers like the Joad family to crushing poverty. In George Orwell's *Nineteen Eighty-Four* it's a different kind of state power: the brutal totalitarian regime run by Big Brother.

> Whatever the source of the antagonist's power, it must be strong enough to force your protagonist to take ever more risky actions to try to overcome the opposition that's keeping them from getting what they want.

People often refer to the antagonist as the "villain." This is not a helpful term for the writer. You have to know and understand what *motivates* your antagonist. Actors know this, know they cannot play a villain, they can only play a person who wants something and takes action to try to get it. After all, the antagonist might be a respected member of the community, might even be the protagonist's friend, or relative, husband, or lover. Tolstoy put this dynamic perfectly when he said: "The best stories don't come from good vs. bad but from good vs. good."

So, concentrate on what drives your antagonist. For the purposes of your story, the essential thing about the antagonist is that they must remain implacable. That is, they must never stop going after what they want. If they do, your story ends.

Having said how important a strong antagonist is, we'll next turn our focus to your protagonist, because this is the character who must engage the reader most personally and most deeply. Your protagonist is your story's soul. It's their struggle you're telling. And that is at the heart of every page-turner.

.

CHAPTER 3

MAKE US CARE

"The novelist who refuses sentiment refuses the full spectrum of human behavior, and then he just dries up. Irony is always scratching your tired ass, whatever way you look at it. I would rather give full vent to all human loves and disappointments, and take a chance on being corny, than die a smartass."

JIM HARRISON

CREATING YOUR STORY'S PROTAGONIST

For the writer, Job Number One is creating an engaging protagonist, someone who causes the events of a stirring story. It's this person's tale you're telling. Their struggle drives the narrative.

> Never forget that our overarching task as writers is to create an emotional response in the reader.

Emotion is how we understand things deeply; it's how our brains work. Abstractions don't move us; emotional experiences do. We are hard-wired this way. That's why telling stories is humanity's most profound way of communicating. Whether it's the preacher who gives an inspiring sermon, or the mother who tells her kids about Grandpa's adventures in the war, or the demagogue who incites a crowd, or the guy at the office who keeps everyone entertained around the proverbial water-cooler, it's all storytelling, and story is always about evoking emotion. I believe that we human beings are not thinking creatures who can feel; we are feeling creatures who can think.

> For you as a writer, this means creating a protagonist who elicits a strong emotional response, a character the reader cares about. It boils down to one crucial quality. Empathy.

EMPATHY VS. SYMPATHY

The essential characteristic of your protagonist is that they elicit the reader's empathy, but they don't necessarily have to elicit sympathy. What's the difference? Sympathy means "I feel for you. I'm sorry for you." Empathy means "I feel *with* you. I identify." Sympathetic also means "likable," but empathetic means "like me." It means that deep down in that character, even an unlikable character, the reader recognizes a core of shared humanity.

I'm not talking about altruism; we empathize for very personal reasons. A good example is Scarlett O'Hara, the heroine of Margaret Mitchell's civil war saga *Gone With the Wind*. Scarlett is a vain, spoiled, selfish young woman, but someone the reader comes to care deeply about. Another example is Don Corleone, the mafia boss in Mario Puzo's novel *The Godfather*. I like referring to these two novels, because both were blockbuster books that were made into blockbuster movies, so most people are familiar with the stories. And they are wonderful stories.

In *The Godfather* Don Corleone is not a nice person. As a mafia leader he bribes judges, he buys politicians, he has people murdered. Yet we empathize with him. Why? After all, intellectually we know we should loathe him for his criminal activities. Instead, we empathize, because Mario Puzo carefully and skillfully shows him to us in ways that will make us care. Puzo does this in three ways.

First, in the big wedding scene near the opening in which Don Corleone's daughter is getting married, we see him as a devoted and loving father, surrounded by affectionate friends and family, a man to whom family and community are paramount. We warm to that. We can identify with that.

Second, Puzo shows us that the Don uses violence against his enemies only when he's pushed to, after he's been hurt first. We unconsciously forgive him for that, and, again, we identify instinctively. Hurt me and I'll strike back too.

Third, we never actually *see* Don Corleone hurting anyone; he does his dark deeds "off-stage." So, although we know intellectually that he uses violence, we don't see it and therefore we don't *feel* it. Whereas we are shown, very graphically, the violence that the Don's enemies do to him and those he loves, like when his son Santino (Sonny) is gunned down. That, we see. We experience it, so we feel the Don's pain and grief. We empathize.

Equally important, Don Corleone is shown to have the respect, even the awe, of people around him. The novel begins with short vignettes of men who need personal favors for the welfare of their families. For example, one wants vengeance on the would-be rapists who beat his daughter so badly she's been hospitalized. These men come to the Don because he can help them. *That* is the source of his power. People look up to the godfather as though he really were a god. This gives him great stature, and stature too confers empathy. I suspect it's because we would all love to have the respect and admiration of our friends, so we transfer our good feeling about that to Don Corleone. Even as he crushes his enemies, he is empathetic.

Scarlett O'Hara is an equally brilliant literary creation. Margaret Mitchell took ten years to write *Gone With the Wind*. It was published in 1936 and was an immediate bestseller. Then, one day, as she was crossing Peachtree Street in Atlanta, a taxi-cab hit her, killing her. But her single novel lives on, one of the best-loved books of all time. And one of the most skillfully constructed.

How does Mitchell get us to care about a vain, self-absorbed, selfish young woman like Scarlett O'Hara? Partly, it's because we get to see Scarlett's passions so deeply. Even if we don't approve of her, we understand her, we "get" her being in love almost to the point of obsession, because most of us have been deeply in love and know how that affects and changes us.

And, partly, our empathy for Scarlett grows because other people, truly good people, feel real affection for her. Mammy likes her. Scarlett's father loves her, and so does her saintly mother, Ellen. Even Melanie, Scarlett's rival for Ashley's love, has warm feelings for Scarlett. So the reader feels a natural human response. If other people—good people—like this young woman, there must be something worthwhile about her.

Finally, we empathize with Scarlett because she is such a forceful, willful person. There's not a moment in this big saga in which she is passive. Scarlett inevitably takes action. Eventually, we get to know Scarlett almost as well as ourselves, and that creates the greatest empathy, but long before that, even when she is selfish and scheming, we can't help admiring her because she's just so damned determined.

A final example of an unlikely character being empathetic is Major Georges Picquart, the well-educated army officer who is the protagonist in Robert Harris's historical thriller *An Officer and a Spy*. Set in 1895 in Paris, the book highlights the famous, true conviction of Alfred Dreyfus for espionage and his exile to the hellhole prison of Devil's Island. The novel begins with Major Picquart reporting to the generals at the War Office about Dreyfus's imminent departure to serve out his prison sentence. Picquart is a coolly aloof man, an admirer of fine art and music, indifferent to Dreyfus's declaration of innocence and his incarceration. So, in these first few pages Picquart is not a very likeable protagonist. And yet, in his very feelings of superiority to the spy we can identify with him for two reasons: first, because he is a sincerely loyal officer—the army is his life; and second, because who of us has not accepted what our authorities tell us when that's all the information we're given? But Picquart has a streak of obstinacy that makes him dig for the truth, discover that Dreyfus is innocent, and then speak out even as he faces mounting threats to his career from the generals, and, eventually, threats to his life. Picquart's gradual transformation from detached indifference to a passionate commitment to righting a miscarriage of justice creates potent empathy in the reader.

FIVE TIPS FOR BUILDING EMPATHY

As you construct your novel, you'll carefully build up and enrich the empathy for your protagonist, using specific techniques that I'll discuss later. But first, here are six ways you can create *instant* empathy.

Tip #1. Make her good at her job.

Whether she's a surgeon, a music teacher, a spy, a renaissance painter, an astronaut, or a butterfly collector, we all admire anyone who does their job well. In the film *The Professional* the protagonist, played by Jean Reno, is a hit man named Leon. He's very good at his job: murder. Again, just as in *The Godfather*, we don't see Leon kill anyone (he does that offstage), while what we *do* see is a tidy, quiet, well-mannered bachelor. At the film's beginning we see him take pleasure in lavishing care on a house plant, nurturing it with water and sunlight. Later, he extends that care to a frightened, threatened orphan (played by the twelve-year-old Natalie Portman). My point is that even before that protective relationship unfolds, the viewer feels respect, even a touch of admiration, for this outlaw simply because he is a cool and careful expert in his field.

Tip #2. Give him a sense of humor.

I don't mean he's a stand-up comic, or even a guy who makes wisecracks. I mean he's someone who can smile about life. We all warm to such people. The appeal of a character with a wry twist on life is so foolproof, it can be used in extraordinarily inventive ways, as Mark Haddon does in his novel *The Curious Incident of the Dog in the Night-Time.* Christopher, the book's autistic boy narrator, tells us that "This will not be a funny book. I cannot tell jokes because I do not understand them." But it's not so: everything Christopher tells us and shows us is tinged with his unique "take" on the world, an attitude that's so fresh, we smile.

Tip #3. Make her the victim of undeserved misfortune.

For example, she's fired in a corporate cutback, or ridiculed for her appearance, or loses a loved one. In Stephen King's novel *Carrie,* the eponymous seventeen-year-old heroine's unfashionable clothes and clumsiness make her the constant target of her schoolmates' mockery and practical jokes. And what reader doesn't cheer when Carrie turns the tables on her tormentors?

Tip #4. Put him in physical jeopardy.

This will always make us care, but be careful with it; don't have him a passive victim. We may feel sorry for him, but to really engage us, to make us feel empathy, he's got to take action using some kind of resourcefulness to get himself *out* of jeopardy.

Tip #5. Give her everyday flaws.

Even if she's a super-competent professional, such as a surgeon or lawyer, maybe she forgets people's names. Even if she's a skilled

FBI investigator, maybe she always trips on the same bedroom stair. Giving her everyday foibles like these will humanize her.

Tip #6. Have them help someone else.

This is an especially effective way to build empathy for a character who, at the start of the story, is a loner. This was the case with the heroine, Alana Marks, in my novel *The Experiment*. Alana was born into a Roma (gypsy) family in New York City, making her an outsider in the mainstream world, and she makes her living as a movie stuntwoman, a career that's far from normal. To illustrate this technique of "helping someone else" here's an abridged excerpt from *The Experiment*. (Note, too, how it uses the "good at her job" technique.) This excerpt occurs half-way through the chapter that introduces Alana. She is in the middle of a film shoot, standing at the open door of a barn loft, about to do a gag (the term the pros use for "stunt") in which the crew will set the rear of the barn ablaze and Alana will set herself on fire and jump out. Here is the excerpt:

> She stood on the lip of the loft, checking everything one last time. She and the crew had already been through an intensive cue-to-cue rehearsal, but a high fall plus full body burn was not something she undertook lightly. Beneath her Civil War period nightgown she wore a fire retardant suit, and under that a protective film of Nomex gel. Her skin tingled with the cold, because she kept her Nomex on ice; it helped against the heat of the burn. There was fire retardant on her wig, too; it was her bare feet she was concerned

about. Still, they were freezing from the gel, so that reassured her.

She looked down at the box rig she would fall onto forty feet below, satisfied at how she and her crew had stacked the layers of folded cardboard boxes. She mentally ran through the mid-air rotation she would do ... Below, the crew were setting up the dolly shot. Gaffers hauled electrical cables, and grips pushed the camera along the track, rehearsing the shot, while the director and the AD discussed it. The fire extinguishers stood ready near the box rig. She trusted the guys to reach her fast. They'd better—on fire, she wouldn't have any air to breathe until they put out the flames. She felt a small shiver, knowing the liquid nitrogen would feel cold as hell, but so very welcome.

"All set up there, sweetheart?" the AD called.

"You bet," she called down. She gave him a clear thumbs-up.

"Okay, people," he announced to the crew, "let's get this in the can."

Alana felt the familiar adrenaline rush: a hot spike of fear bathed by cold confidence. It was a sweet thrill, and she knew it would get sweeter. She held the igniter in the folds of her nightgown, ready to set herself ablaze. She was prepared.

The crew set the rear of the barn alight, and the cameras rolled. Alana could hear the flames' faint crackle far behind her. Now, all eyes were on her. All the lights too. She turned her head to "play away," not let the cameras see that her face wasn't the starlet's she was doubling for.

Something was wrong. Her peripheral vision caught a movement inside on the barn floor. Beyond the lit-up shelf of the loft, it was dark down there. As she focused on a spot among the shadowy straw bales, her breath caught. A man lay in the straw. Gus? He'd been her safety inside the barn for the cue-to-cue, and he must have stayed there and passed out. Drunk again.

She could have killed him. She'd met Gus Yuill back when he was a top stuntman, and she probably owed him her life, but he'd let booze ruin him ... *Screw Gus. He's not my responsibility. Let the drunk burn.*

Flames crackled nearer. She smelled smoke, heard voices, Ian's and the AD's, yelling up at her: "Jump! Now!"

She saw Gus struggling to sit up among the bales, coughing at the smoke. It rocked her to her senses. That she'd considered, even for a second, letting him die! Gus had taken her in off the street when she was fifteen, trained her, given her her first job. Of *course* she had to save him. But now the problem hit her. If she alerted the AD to haul him out, they'd see how wasted he was and he'd never work again. She couldn't let that happen either.

She had an idea.

"Abort!" she called down. "I've made a mistake."

"You *what*?" the AD yelled.

"Let my gel get too dry. Can't do it. Abort!"

"Oh, fuck … " He sounded freaked. He yelled for the crew to put out the fire, and barked an order over his radio to the fire truck.

The director burst out, "What the hell? No, we're not cutting! Do the jump, Alana! Just *do* it!" But she was already on the ladder going down from the loft to the interior. She heard the pandemonium outside. The AD: "If she says she can't we gotta stop!" And the furious director: "Jesus fucking Christ … yeah, yeah, cut … put out the fire. *Fuck* this!" And Ian's irate voice punching through: "Alana, get your ass out here!"

She reached Gus among the straw bales. Coughing, bleary-eyed, he looked up at her in bewilderment. The smoke was so strong it stung her eyes. She slung his limp arm around her neck. "Dumb old fart. Let's go. Hold on to me."

She dragged him out the back door and they made it into the adjacent woods just as crew swarmed around the barn with fire extinguishers, and the fire truck roared up. As the crew sprang into action putting out the flames, Alana prayed that no one could see her and Gus crouching in the trees, catching their breath.

He flopped onto his back in the dry leaves. His voice came out wobbly, but with his roguish laugh. "Holy shit."

Although Alana's lifestyle is foreign to the reader, making it a challenge to identify with her as the book begins, this action of hers to help Gus, however reluctantly, immediately humanizes her and builds our empathy for her.

The Long Game

There's one more reason why it's so important to create a protagonist with whom we empathize. This person has to be someone the reader will want to spend time with, spend a whole book with.

It's very different than a movie. For one thing, an audience's experience is passive—you sit back and let the film wash over you; nothing is required of you—whereas with a book, the reader's mind must work, a partner in creation. For another, there's so much to visually captivate a film viewer: spirited actors, spectacular special effects, fascinating locations like a South Sea isle or the interior of a submarine at war. Such images can dazzle a viewer into watching a film no matter how weak the story or how cardboard the characters. Also, a movie lasts for just an hour and a half.

Not so with a novel. The reader has to make an investment of time that's far longer, and that requires real commitment. If watching a film is a one-night stand, enjoying a novel is a long-term love affair. This means that at the outset the reader has to feel confident they're going to like spending a long time with the main character. An ineffectual or passive protagonist is not going to inspire that kind of confidence.

So, even if your protagonist isn't exactly heroic, make him or her someone who, from the very beginning, is loyal or clever or hardworking or just oddly fascinating—some quality that instantly sparks a warm reaction or a quiver of curiosity in the reader and makes them want to stay for the long haul.

Six Essentials

There are six essential elements in the creation of a protagonist who will kindle durable empathy in the reader. They are:

- A conscious desire put into action
- High stakes
- Close relationships
- Motivation
- Consistency plus contradiction
- A pressing issue besides the main plot

1. A Conscious Desire Put into Action

Author Kurt Vonnegut taught his creative writing students to "have your character want something right away, even if it's just a glass of water." That's excellent advice. And I suggest going even further. Readers care about a protagonist who wants something, and knows it, and actively tries to get it. Passive characters—that is, characters who are introspective to the point of inaction—cannot drive a compelling novel. Over two thousand years ago Aristotle defined this concept, saying that drama is not a portrayal of character but rather of action.

> Make your protagonist a willful being, someone who wants or needs something and takes action to try to get it.

The actions they take then bring them into direct conflict with people around them, whether it's a single mother struggling to keep her family together, or a rooky detective who must stop a killer from striking again. And the actions they take must produce meaningful consequences that escalate the conflict.

In all good novels the protagonist has a conscious desire. In superior novels they also have an unconscious desire, some yearning that, although unknown to the character at the start, is even stronger. The realization of their newly understood self often propels the climax. In Jane Austen's *Emma*, Emma discovers, at the story climax, that Mr. Knightely, the man she has always believed was nothing more to her than a trusted family friend, is really the man she loves with all her heart. In Khaled Hosseini's *The Kite Runner,* Amir discovers that instead of continuing to cover up his many sins, as he has for years, he feels compelled to risk everything to save his dead brother's son. He wants to be good.

This unconscious desire is the hero or heroine's spiritual journey. The most memorable protagonists are on a spiritual journey even if they don't know it. The events of the novel bring them to an awakening. They discover something profound about themselves and their world.

2. High Stakes

What your central character is striving for should involve high stakes. The book's main conflict will increase in tension because of these stakes. They may not be fate-of-the-world stakes; if they are, like in a Tom Clancy thriller, that's fine, but it's not necessary. What *is* necessary is that the stakes are supremely important *to the character*. Though actual life-and-death risks may not be involved, the situation must *feel* that way to them.

Here's an example. Maeve Binchy's novel *Scarlet Feather* begins with Cathy Scarlet, having just launched a catering business, on her way to cater the New Year's Eve party for her wealthy mother-in-law, Hannah, who looks down on Cathy, the daughter of her maid. Cathy is keyed-up because she wants so much to shine in the eyes of her powerful mother-in-law. She also wants to prove herself to her husband, a busy lawyer who doesn't take her business seriously, considering it just a hobby. So, for Cathy, the stakes are very high. She and her fledgling company need this success, and she knows Hannah can break her. We feel for Cathy, and we're eager to find out: will she succeed? She does, for a while, and then the book's second half increases the stakes for her when a theft inside her catering business forces her to fight for its survival.

3. Close Relationships

So many great stories are family stories. From *Pride and Prejudice* to *War and Peace* to *The Grapes of Wrath,* unforgettable stories revolve around tight family relationships. We care about people who are deeply involved with other people.

In *Pride and Prejudice,* Jane Austen created her classic, sparkling love story between Elizabeth Bennett and Mr. Darcy, but some of Elizabeth's moments of deepest feeling—which generate our deepest empathy with her—come from her profound concern about her own family. There is first her distress for her beloved elder sister, Jane, having her heart broken by Bingley, and later the terrible disgrace that her younger sister, Lydia, brings on the entire family by eloping with Wickham. And, in between those points of emotional intensity, we also feel Elizabeth's warm affection for her sardonic father, who adores her, and her acute embarrassment at the gauche behavior of her mother (something we can all identify with, because who of us does not remember, as teenagers, being embarrassed by a parent?). These family relationships form the continuous heartbeat of Elizabeth's story. They are what make her the most "real" to us.

In John Steinbeck's masterpiece *The Grapes of Wrath*, Tom Joad's story unfolds in the blighted landscape and violent turmoil of the Great Depression, and he fights as best he can against these stacked odds, but it is the unshakable bonds of family relationships that forge Tom's soul, and our genuine empathy, as he strives for survival alongside his parents, grandparents, sisters and brothers. Again, family interactions are paramount.

Donna Tartt's Pulitzer Prize-winning novel *The Goldfinch* is a web of tightly strung family relationships for teenager Theo Decker. First, we see Theo's affectionate attachment to his vivacious mother. After her death, he is horribly betrayed by his deadbeat dad. And he forges a life-changing friendship with his mercurial, brilliant, druggie pal Boris, who becomes closer than a brother, though a brother Theo isn't sure he can really trust.

Giving your characters close family ties produces not only drama in itself, it also allows the reader to empathize instantly, because we all live in family situations awash with emotional currents, both positive and negative.

Let's say you're writing about a young man who is in debt with crushing student loans, desperate to find work. We'll call him Tony. He's been looking for a job for months, sending out résumés, knocking on doors, making cold calls, all with no luck. But he's hardworking and determined and finally lands a job, a good one. Then, someone in the company undermines Tony and steals his job. Now, if that someone is a stranger, sure we'll feel sorry for Tony. But what if the person who steals his job is his own brother? Now we really empathize, because there are layers of personal history here, layers of tension.

Conflict from the most trivial to the most serious, when it occurs between characters who have close ties by blood or marriage, magnifies and intensifies what's at stake for both parties. It adds personal tension to the characters' confrontations, making your story more powerful.

Some stories simply can't center around family ties. In John Grisham's *The Firm*, his protagonist, Mitch, works at a law firm that he discovers is run by the mafia. Grisham perhaps decided that he couldn't impose family relationships there. But, notice that he gives Mitch two intense family ties. One is with his wife Abby, his best friend and confidante, and the second is with his beloved older brother, Ray, who's in prison. Grisham also has these two characters play pivotal roles in building to the story's climax.

If blood ties are impossible between the characters in your story, try at least to give them intense relationships through friendship or love. For example: a couple in a long-standing love affair; men who were comrades at war; women who've been best friends since they were five; workers who are the closest of colleagues. Close ties like any of these will yield richly dramatic results in your story.

4. *Motivation*

To make the reader *really* care about your protagonist, you must expose their deepest motivation: what they most want, fear, need. Their secret desires, their strongest loves, their darkest hates. Their terrors, joys, anxieties, and longings—both in the present, and also for the future. This illumination of a character's interior life bares their very soul, and draws the reader close.

For this depiction of a character's interior life, I like using a word borrowed from the language of poetry criticism: *inscape.*

> Just as a landscape depicts the detail and spirit of a place, a character's inscape is their inner life laid bare. Their secret life.

To illustrate this, let's look at excerpts from two brilliant novels. Each features a character lying in bed alone, consumed with love, though the two are vastly different personalities. Note how intimately we see their unique, inmost thoughts.

The first excerpt, slightly abridged, is from Ian McEwan's *Atonement,* set during World War II. Robbie is a young man who grew up poor but intends to be a doctor. He and the well-to-do Cecilia have been friends since childhood, but an event occurs at the book's opening—a childish tussle over a vase that falls into a fountain and breaks—and this seemingly insignificant event jolts Robbie into the electric realization that he's crazy in love with Cecilia. The flashpoint for him was when she stripped down to her underwear to retrieve the vase. Here's the excerpt that bares Robbie's soul:

He stretched out on the bed, face down into his pillow, and groaned. The sweetness of her, the delicacy, his childhood friend, and now in danger of becoming unreachable. To strip off like that—yes, her endearing attempt to seem eccentric, her stab at being bold had an exaggerated, homemade quality. Now she would be in agonies of regret, and could not know what she had done to him. And all of this would be very well, it would be rescuable, if she was not so angry with him over a broken vase that had come apart in his hands. But he loved her fury too … He returned to what was real: she was angry with him, and she would be angrier still when she knew he was to be one of the dinner guests. Out there, in the fierce light, he hadn't thought quickly enough to refuse Leon's invitation. Automatically, he had bleated out his yes, and now he would face her irritation. He groaned again, and didn't care if he were heard downstairs, at the memory of how she had taken off her clothes in front of him—so indifferently, as though he were an infant. Of course. He saw it now. The idea was to humiliate him. There it stood, the undeniable fact. Humiliation. She wanted it for him. She was not mere sweetness, and he could not afford to condescend to her, for she was a force, she could drive him out of his depth and push him under …

This torture was his punishment for breaking her ridiculous vase. He should never see her again. He had to see her tonight. He had no choice anyway—he was going. She would despise him for coming. He should have refused Leon's invitation, but the moment it was made his pulse had leaped and his bleated yes had left his mouth. He'd be in a room with her tonight, and the body he had seen, the moles, the pallor, the strawberry mark, would be concealed inside her clothes. He alone would know ... And Cecilia would not speak or look at him. Even that would be better than lying here groaning. No, it wouldn't. It would be worse, but still he wanted it. He had to have it. He wanted it to be worse.

We see so deeply into Robbie's longings and fears that we almost ache along with him.

The second example is an excerpt, also slightly abridged, from *Gone With the Wind*, Margaret Mitchell's classic saga of the American Civil War. Scarlett O'Hara is sixteen years old and besotted with the dashing Ashley Wilkes. Like Robbie in the excerpt above, Scarlett is lying in bed alone, fired by longing, but she is determined, and she has a plan:

Somehow she would maneuver to get a few minutes alone with him, away from the crowd. She hoped everything would work out that way, because it would be more difficult otherwise. But if Ashley didn't make the first move she would simply have to do it herself.

When they were finally alone he would have fresh in his mind the picture of the other men thronging about her, he would be newly impressed with the fact that every one of them wanted her, and that look of sadness and despair would be in his eyes. Then she would make him happy again by letting him discover that, popular though she was, she preferred him above every man in all the world. And when she admitted it, modestly and sweetly, she would look a thousand things more. Of course, she would do it all in a ladylike way. She wouldn't even dream of saying to him boldly that she loved him—that would never do. But the manner of telling him troubled her not at all. She had managed such situations before and she could do it again.

Why, by this time tomorrow night she might be Mrs. Ashley Wilkes!

She sat up in bed, hugging her knees, and for a long happy, moment she *was* Mrs. Ashley Wilkes—Ashley's bride! Then a slight chill entered her heart. Suppose it didn't work out this way? Suppose Ashley didn't beg her to run away with him? Resolutely, she pushed the thought from her mind.

"I won't think of that now," she said firmly. "If I think of it now, it will upset me. There's no reason why things won't come out the way I want them—if he loves me. And I know he does!"

We see so clearly this girl's determined spirit that, almost despite ourselves, we hope she gets what she wants.

You can also lead the reader to care about a character by showing their self-awareness. Once again, Scarlett O'Hara is a good example. Just when we think we know this girl—vain, self-absorbed, spoiled rotten—we see, through her thoughts, how she adores and reveres her mother, Ellen. Ellen is refined, gentle, generous, and compassionate; everything that Scarlett is not. Scarlett knows this about herself, and she sees her mother almost as a saint. In fact, when Scarlett was very little she used to confuse her mother with the Virgin Mary. Nothing pleases Scarlett as much as Ellen's praise. Margaret Mitchell did this for a reason. She made Scarlett aware that she'll never be as good as her mother, and this humanizes Scarlett. However annoying and infuriating Scarlett is, we like her for knowing her own shortcomings.

> The more self-aware your protagonist is, the more stature they have in the reader's eyes.

You can see from the above excerpts how potent this revealing of a character's inscape is, and yet new writers often omit it in their manuscripts. It's as if they see a film playing out in their heads and expect the reader to see the same film. But a novel is not a movie. In a movie, the actor is a living canvas, *showing* the character's inscape. But in a novel, if a character is involved in some action that significantly affects them—for example, they witness a murder—and the author leaves out all reference to that character's thoughts and feelings about what happened, the reader sees that character as an oddly blank personality. When I pointed this out to a young writer I was mentoring, he said, "Oh, I thought what she went through was so big, her feelings would be obvious." They're not. In fact, it's the opposite. If we see a character's mind and heart as a blank slate, our response is: how can she be so cold, so unmoved?

> A novel is not a movie. You, the author, have to do the work of the actor, sharing the character's thoughts and feelings.

5. Consistency with Contradiction

This technique plays with an intriguing paradox. Your protagonist needs to be consistent. I don't mean predictable or stereotypical, I mean that characters, like real people, have a core personality that defines them. How unsettling would it be if every time you visited a friend she yawned at topics that had previously enthralled her, was spellbound by things that had never interested her before, had a complete change of attitude about politics and religion? You might think she needed serious professional help. If characters deviate excessively from their core personality they come across as unrealistic, not making sense.

But here's the paradox. To flesh out a character—to bring them to life—it pays to give an edge to that consistency with a contradiction. In my thriller *Entrapped* the central character is a corporate lawyer who is ultra-competent, conservative, very much in control. That's her core personality. So, here's the contradiction I added to humanize her: when she's tense, she relaxes by smoking a little weed.

You can find paradoxes like this in just about everyone close to you. My late father was a family doctor. He stitched up wounds, set broken bones, snipped tonsils, delivered babies. Highly capable, right? But here's the contradiction: that man could not use a household tool without hurting himself. If you gave him a screwdriver, he'd cut himself. God forbid you give him a saw! When my husband and I were building our house, Dad often came on weekends to lend a hand along with my brothers, and after a few weeks, whenever someone wanted to know where Dad was, we'd joke: "Just follow the trail of blood."

Adding contradictory details like these gives your characters an intriguing reality that will leave your readers nodding in recognition, feeling, "Yup, that's weird but so true."

6. Issues Beyond the Main Plot

You can enliven your protagonist further, and reveal a lot about them, by having them deal with some everyday issue apart from the pressing dilemma of the main plot. Give them at least one ordinary, down-to-earth problem as an ongoing plot thread. A demanding boss, for example. Or a charming friend who's in trouble. Or a sick relative. Even a recurring toothache. Problems like these will anchor your protagonist in the concrete, workaday world, and thus enhance their humanity. Be careful not to let such minor plot threads take over and choke out your main plot, but do weave them throughout the main plot whenever possible. In *Entrapped* my protagonist, the hard-nosed corporate lawyer Liv Gardner, faces a central dilemma of violent sabotage against her company's oil wells and she acts with no-holds-barred toughness, and so, to reveal her gentler side, I gave her the side-problem of a schizophrenic sister whom she loves, a pretty younger sister who's forever sleeping with guys she shouldn't, and forgetting to take her meds, so Liv has to constantly watch out for her and protect her.

Make use of this technique strategically. What "strategic" means is that when you choose to add an issue besides the main plot, don't make the choice arbitrary or random, but one that has thematic consistency with your story. Robert McKee calls theme the "controlling idea," a phrase I like because it emphasizes that you, the writer, are in control of all the choices you make. For example, the controlling idea of *Entrapped* is "Power corrupts, until we use it to do good." Liv Gardner uses her power to entrap her enemy, until her feeling for him is challenged and changed, so my choice of a side-issue with thematic consistency—a kind of counterpoint about power—was to give her a powerless sister she has to protect.

By developing all the above elements in creating your story's protagonist, you'll imbue that person with richly human qualities, forging a bond with your readers that's the purpose of every page-turner.

Deep Character

Now, to broaden our examination of the empathetic protagonist, let's look at what I call Deep Character. There are four facets of Deep Character: characterization, choice, change, and contrast.

Characterization

Characterization is the surface of Deep Character; it's all the externals. These include the character's gender, age, physical characteristics, heritage, occupation, marital status, social status,

IQ, education; their choice of home, car, clothes; their outward personality and even their public attitudes. In other words, this covers everything that you might take note of in an acquaintance; for example in a new neighbor if you watched them carefully for a few weeks, taking notes. All of this is called characterization, and you must know it about the central characters in your book. It's helpful to "interview" your protagonist and ask them the following kinds of questions:

- Of her friends and family, who is she closest to? Who does she *wish* she were closest to?
- What does he do when he's angry?
- What's her biggest fear? Who has she told this to? Who would she never tell this to?
- What makes him laugh?
- Has she ever been in love? Had her heart broken?
- What's in his refrigerator right now? What's on his nightstand?
- When she thinks of her childhood kitchen, what smell does she associate with it? Sauerkraut? Oatmeal cookies? Paint? Beer? Why is the smell so resonant for her?
- He's getting ready for a night out. Where is he going? Who will he be with?
- What's their fondest memory? Their wildest dream? Proudest moment? Secret indulgence? Latest purchase?

All of the above is good information for you to know about your protagonist. But it is not Deep Character. In the most compelling stories, characters are never what they seem at the start; the story is about how they reveal themselves.

> No matter what characters say, or
> how they comport themselves, the
> only way we ever come to know them
> in depth is by the choices they make
> under pressure.

Choice

Choice under pressure reveals deep character. We see it all the time in real life. The guy everyone discounts as a quiet, timid soul, but when he's sent off to war and faces soul-testing pressure, he performs a brave act of self sacrifice that saves his whole platoon. The drug-addicted teenage girl living on the streets who gets pregnant, and then surprises everyone by becoming a capable and loving mother. The respected, wealthy CEO, a pillar of the community, who gets hooked on gambling and his debts drive him to embezzle from his own company.

So, for the writer creating a compelling protagonist, here's a helpful definition:

> True character—deep character—is
> revealed by the choices a person makes
> under pressure in pursuit of their desire.

To illustrate this, let's imagine a woman from New York who flies to Africa on business, to Abuja, the capitol of Nigeria. Let's call her Lois. She checks into her hotel room for a good night's sleep, and when she wakes up the next morning there's been a revolution, a coup. The government has fled, the rebels have taken over, the city is in chaos. Lois has two choices. She can get on the last plane out to New York, or she can stay. The obvious choice is to get out. But, what if the reason she came to Abuja is to patch things up with her estranged sister, Kate, who's an aid worker, and now Kate has been taken hostage by the rebels? (Remember: whenever possible, use family relationships.) Now, does Lois go or stay? Either choice will reveal something very deep about her.

Does the type of pressure matter? Yes. The greater the pressure, the deeper the revelation. For example, a woman planning a dinner party can feel pressure, and she has to make lots of choices: the guests, the food, the wine, the seating arrangements, what to wear. But we've all been there and we know it's hardly a crisis. I'm bored just telling you about it. These are not choices to build a story on.

In contrast, imagine a woman in a World War II concentration camp. She has two young children and she is forced to decide which one will live and which will die. That's a choice so agonizing, it's almost as unbearable for the reader as for the character. And that's exactly the horrific dilemma William Styron gave his protagonist in his wrenching novel *Sophie's Choice*. The type and degree of pressure matter.

What does this mean for you, the writer? It means *use* the principle to make strategic choices in your writing. Create situations that put your protagonist under the most extreme pressure as they pursue their goals. Their choices under pressure will reveal their deep character.

Change

Many of the greatest stories are about transformation. Ebenezer Scrooge in Charles Dickens's *A Christmas Carol* is a cold-hearted, pitiless miser who shuts out everyone around him, but when visiting spirits force him to see the heart-wrenching, missed opportunities in his life, the experience transforms him into a gregarious philanthropist, generous employer, and affectionate uncle. His transformation is so profound it has become a timeless emotional touchstone for our culture, because Scrooge personifies the inspiring concept that each of us has the capacity to change and become good.

In *The Kite Runner*, author Khaled Hosseini gives us the story of Amir through the war and turbulence in Afghanistan from the 1970s to the 1990s. Amir, a coward and a liar who betrayed and ruined his friend, unaware that it was his brother, is eventually transformed into a brave man who risks his life to save his brother's son. It's a stunning tale of guilt and redemption.

A protagonist who does not change is boring. They're just repeating predictable behaviors. Such a person may be credible in real life; people who don't change are common. In fact, I would venture to say that *most* people don't change. But a novel is not life; it's a metaphor for life. We read stories to see characters confront hard problems, learn, and be transformed.

Again, Scarlett O'Hara in Margaret Mitchell's *Gone With The Wind* offers a fine example. When we first see sixteen-year-old Scarlett she is naive, self-centered, and pampered. Her whole existence is flirtation in her small, sheltered world, and she knows nothing of the harsh real world. She is a hothouse magnolia. Then war comes, putting immense pressures on Scarlett. Under these pressures, Scarlett's real character begins to reveal itself by the choices she makes. First, as the Union army burns the city of Atlanta around her, and its inhabitants flee, Scarlett stays to single-handedly deliver Melanie's baby, saving the life of both mother and child. Scarlett then battles her way through enemy lines with the sick Melanie and the baby to get back home to Tara. Finding Tara in ruins, Scarlett saves its inhabitants from starvation by forcing everyone, including herself, to do back-breaking labor in the cotton fields. She rebuilds the plantation, and eventually creates a commercial family empire. Not bad for a spoiled little flirt. At the book's end Scarlett is still self-centered, but events have changed her profoundly. She is forged steel.

Contrast

In a way, this is a continuation of the principle above about change, but I want to emphasize again that degree matters. Revelation of true character that is in contrast to characterization is fundamental to all great stories. The point here is that the more extreme the contrast, the more cathartic and satisfying for the reader.

A good example is Michael Corleone in Mario Puzo's novel *The Godfather,* set in New York after World War Two. Michael is the son of Italian mafia boss Don Corleone, the eponymous godfather. When we see Michael at the beginning of the book he's a well-educated young man who has served with distinction in the war and is ready to settle down. He wants no part in his father's underworld business. He loves and respects his father, but he plans a middle-class life for himself in some professional career that's completely different from his father's trade. Also, he loves Kay, a well-educated WASP girl, and plans to marry her. Then, events occur that put extreme pressure on Michael. His father's enemies attack, forcing Michael to make quick, hard choices. He does. First, he risks his life to save his father's life. Then he kills two of his father's enemies, an act that forces

Michael to go into exile in Sicily. There, he falls instantly in love with an earthy, illiterate peasant girl, Apollonia, who is the complete opposite of Kay, and overnight he marries her. Then, Apollonia is murdered by his family's enemies. And back in New York they murder Michael's brother. Michael, a changed man, returns home, faced with pulling together his demoralized clan. When his father dies, Michael takes over, and he goes after his enemies with one well-planned, massive, murderous strike. Michael is transformed. He has become the Godfather—he has become everything he thought he never wanted to be. This is his deep character, his true character. This is wonderful storytelling.

There is a false notion that a hero must be powerful or inordinately brave or clever—some kind of "super" person. It's not so. The crucial dramatic function of a hero is to learn. They may be reluctant to face the teaching, may even have to be dragged kicking and screaming into the lessons, but they will learn, and be changed by it, even to the point of being willing to sacrifice themselves.

> The stories that move us most show transformation of the hero, whether from weakness to strength, or from isolation to inclusion, or from ignorance to wisdom, however hard-won the victory may be.

So, don't hold back. Create a story with events that put such intense pressure on your protagonist, she makes choices that transform her. Do it, and you'll have produced the kind of book readers love and publishers seek. A page-turner.

There is one final technique you should develop in creating a deeply empathetic protagonist. It concerns how you introduce this character, how they first come "on stage." In fact, to explain the dynamic, I'll borrow language from the world of acting.

MAKING AN ENTRANCE

First impressions are crucial. Your initial response when you meet a person gets imprinted on your mind and is hard to alter. This is equally true of a reader's first impression of a character in fiction. Their response at the outset to your story's protagonist is crucial. Yet new writers often waste this opportunity by introducing their protagonist in idleness or passivity. Be smart—put the visceral impact of the first impression to work for you.

Think of your story as a movie, and your protagonist as the star, and give him or her a dynamic and meaningful entrance. Focus on two steps:

1. Determine the character's defining quality.
2. Show that quality through action.

> Action is the key. Description of a character tells the reader mere facts and has little visceral effect, whereas showing the character's defining quality through action creates an emotional response in the reader, leaving a deep and lasting imprint.

Screenwriters do this very consciously. Watch any film you admire and notice how the scene in which the hero or heroine first comes on screen demonstrates their defining quality. In other words, it shows the character's essence.

When actors first read a script this "essence in action" is the very thing they look for. (I know; I made my living as an actor for twenty years.) As a writer of fiction, you can use this screen-writing technique to powerful effect. Strive to write an entrance scene for your protagonist which, if your story were made into a film, would attract an "A-List" actor to the role, a star.

Here are some examples of the kind of dynamic entrance I mean:

1. Meredith Stephure's historical novel *Civil Blood* is set during England's "Glorious Revolution" of 1688. It opens with Thomas de Chastelain, lawyer and loyalist, about to ride off to war, yet he takes a few minutes to deal with a small family crisis: his two bold young sons have been caught trespassing on the neighbor's property. We see Thomas take action to punish the boys, but mildly. Strict but fair, he is full of affection for his children. This is the essence of his character.

2. In A.S. Byatt's novel *Possession,* the ambitious young scholar Roland Mitchell, researching a Victorian poet, opens an old book in the London Library and out fall two unsigned love letters. He's thrilled, sure they were written by the poet. Roland impulsively steals the let-ters—and thus begins his audacious quest to be the first to uncover the truth about his subject. Roland's essence is his drive to excel as the foremost expert in his field.

3. Ian McEwan's novel *Atonement* opens with Briony Tallis, a precocious child, obsessing about the play she

has written and orchestrating her young cousins to take the roles in her fictional world. Her need to control people, and her obsession with storytelling, are the essence of her character.

4. Lee Gowan's *Confession* shows Dwight, a young janitor at an elementary school, breaking up a fight between two boys by lifting the bully up by his shirt and calmly threatening him. Dwight's action shows a man who cares about justice but also carries an aura of latent brutality.

5. My novel *The Queen's Lady*, set in England in the reign of Henry VIII, opens with seven-year-old Honor Larke risking her life to try to find her servant-friend amid a May Day riot. When she sees the mob viciously attack a foreigner, then move on, Honor's curiosity and pity drive her to help the dying stranger. These actions show her essential qualities: loyalty, risk-taking, and compassion.

The examples above are all opening scenes that feature the protagonist, but your opening doesn't have to be about the protagonist. You may want to kick-start the story with some other event, perhaps one featuring the antagonist. What's important is that when you *do* bring your protagonist on stage, give them an entrance in which the action they take shows their essence and resonates on an emotional level with your reader.

To illustrate this principle further, here's an excerpt from my novel *The Queen's Captive*. This scene introduces Honor Thornleigh (née Larke) twenty years after she was first featured in *The Queen's Lady*. In those past years, her radical actions against the church in England forced her and her husband Richard and their children into exile in Antwerp. When I was planning this scene I searched for a way to show, through Honor's actions, two qualities that are the essence of her character: her loyalty to family, and her resourcefulness. Here is the scene I created for her entrance:

> The tavern's low ceiling and rough lumber walls had trapped generations of Antwerp's harborfront smells — fish, stale beer, wet rope and salt-crusted clothes. Boiled turnips, too, Honor Thornleigh thought as she walked quickly through the room. Winter fodder. Staple of the poor. She ate turnips too often these days.
>
> She passed seamen sitting over pots of ale, their desultory talk a stew of many languages — Dutch, Spanish, Portuguese, Italian. One man, dressed in the finer doublet of a ship's master, looked up from his foamy tankard as Honor passed. She lowered her face to hide it behind the edges of her furred hood. She had chosen this sailors' haunt far from her house, but Antwerp's mercantile community was as tight as a gossiping village and she couldn't risk being seen by one of her husband's business associates. Richard had no idea what she was doing behind his back.
>
> She went straight through and out the tavern's back door, and across a cobbled courtyard that stank of gutted fish, where the gusting November wind chased dead, dry leaves. She was relieved to enter the stable with its friendlier smells of hay and horses.

George Mitford was already waiting. He stood at a stall door, scratching the nose of a shaggy bay mare who bowed her head in contentment.

"She seems to love that," Honor said, throwing off her hood.

He smiled when he saw her. "We all love a good scratch."

"Scratch my back, I'll scratch yours?"

"And so the world goes round, my dear."

She gave in to impulse and embraced him. "Thanks to old friends, yes." She paid for her action with a sharp spasm at her rib, cracked by a bullet ten months ago.

"Now, now, don't tease," he said as he pulled back from her embrace. It was his jest, but said with a blush that Honor found endearing, the cheerful fluster of a man who had not forgotten the passionate impulse of youth. She was forty-four and he was ten years older, but he was still fit, still possessed of a thick head of hair though it was sheened with silver. In the old days his hair had been as dark as Honor's was still. Was that really more than two decades ago? He had caught her by the waist under the stairs on Richard's ship as they had sailed into this very harbor, delivering George to safety from the heretic-hunting persecution of the Bishop of London, and in that moment he had fervently declared his love to her. She had laughed. George was not the first man she had rescued whose giddy gratitude had flashed into ardor. "And all I had to do," she'd teased, "was save your life."

Now here he was, saving hers.

She noticed the sturdy case at his feet, a strongbox covered with amber leather secured with studded copper bands and an iron lock. He was never without it. She glanced over her shoulder to make sure she had not been followed. There was no one. Just the soft chomping of horses munching hay, and the keening of wind across the roof's patched holes. She was satisfied that she and George were alone.

She opened her cloak to display the top of her bosom to him, and touched her necklace, an almond-sized emerald pendant on a chain of filigreed gold. The gem was warm against her fingertips, her body's warmth infusing Richard's gift from the summer they were married twenty-one years ago. To her, it held the essence of that sweet summer still. She bent her head to undo the clasp, then handed over the necklace. "I couldn't give it to anyone but you, George."

She saw a moment of deep feeling in his eyes before he lowered his gaze to study the goods. His demeanor was suddenly all business. "Milky inclusion in the left quadrant. Old-fashioned cabochon setting. A nick in the clasp."

Honor winced at the criticism. She loved this necklace, a golden filament with its drop of green fire that connected her to happier days. But she stilled her tongue. George knew how much she needed the cash. He had been buying her jewelry, piece by piece, for months. She glanced down at his leather case, aching with curiosity. Were any of her gems still nestled in the black velvet lining, or did they already adorn his pampered clients? Her ruby earrings that Isabel, as a baby at her breast, had reached out to grab. Her rope of pearls bought on a trip with Richard to Venice. The diamond and sapphire ring he had given her seven years ago after a spectacular wool season. Her brooch of opals and topaz, an heirloom from the mother she had never known—Honor had planned to give it to her stepson Adam's intended at their official betrothal. Her bracelets and necklaces of garnets, carnelian, amber and coral, of lesser value yet cherished all the same. She lifted her eyes from the case, fending off the tug of regret. Her family could not eat rubies and pearls.

As always, George gave her an excellent price. Far better, she knew, than the emerald was worth.

Whether your protagonist is a rogue, a lost soul, a killer, or a saint, use their entrance to make an unforgettable impact. It's your opportunity to make them a star.

PART II

STORY

CHAPTER 4

STORYLINING

"The secret of getting ahead is getting started. The secret of getting started is breaking your complex overwhelming tasks into small manageable tasks, and then starting on the first one."

MARK TWAIN

BUILDING YOUR BOOK FROM OUTLINE TO FINAL DRAFT

I magine an interior designer who takes a basic architectural course that so inspires her she instantly sets out to build a house. She has thrilling ideas for its appearance (after all, she's been admiring fine buildings all her life) and is so eager to get it done and unveil it to the world, she foregoes making blueprints. Blueprints take time, and she's sure they'll deaden her creative flow, so she plunges straight into construction. She throws the walls up, hammers in ceiling joists, and slaps on the roof. With the house now standing, she happily tackles what she *really* likes doing: the decorating. But, while she's enjoying playing with colors and fabrics, a wall begins to crumble. A joist comes loose. The roof sags. She hears creaking and cracking, and soon the house collapses around her.

Crafting a compelling novel takes as much careful construction as building a house, yet inexperienced writers often try to slap a book together without a plan. They're impatient to get to the enjoyable part: playing with words (the decorating). But they may discover that the structure they've built simply won't stand up.

The single most important piece of advice I can give you is: take the time to build an outline.

I call it a storyline. It's a helpful term for writers, partly because the word "outline" sounds clinical and detached, and, more importantly, because we must never forget that we're telling a story. Stories are about life-and-blood people.

> The storyline is where all the heavy lifting of creation gets done. It's where you give life to your characters and craft the plot.

WHAT IS A STORYLINE?

A storyline is a document of about twenty to thirty double-spaced pages that lays out *just what happens*. It's written in prose, not point form; you're writing a narrative. The storyline strips your story down to its bare essentials. This lets you see the places where it's weak, where the characters' relationships lack life, where the action slows and sinks—places where you're going to have to think harder and dig deeper about how to achieve a coherent, compelling tale.

You start with just one paragraph: who your central character is (the protagonist), what their goal is, and their main problem (the central conflict). Then, through several drafts that gradually grow, you build it into a full storyline of around twenty to thirty pages with a beginning, middle, and end.

STORYLINE VS. SYNOPSIS

Here's an important point. Don't confuse a storyline (an outline) with a synopsis. A synopsis is a *sales* tool; it's a public document that you write after your novel is finished. It will be just a couple of pages long, and its purpose is to describe your book in a way that will entice, even excite, a literary agent or an acquisition editor at a publishing house. To reprise my comparison with house construction, a synopsis is the equivalent of a marketing brochure about the house.

A storyline, on the other hand, is a *working* tool; it's for you alone, a private document. It doesn't need to sound enticing, just as a house blueprint doesn't need to look enticing, because no one sees your storyline except you (unless, of course, you're working with a trusted partner such as your agent). The storyline stays on your desk, unseen by others, growing in length through several drafts as you build your story. Only after your book is completely finished and you move into the stage of pitching it to an agent or publisher do you write a synopsis to "sell" it.

Take Time

How long does it take to create a complete storyline? When I'm writing a book I spend three to four months on my storyline while concurrently doing research. I do this even when under contract with my publisher to produce a book a year, as was the case with my Thornleigh Saga series of historical novels. Completing a book in one year is a challenge, but even so, I always spend about four months on the storyline and its associated research. I consider the storylining process that crucial.

You may think four months sounds like a long time to work on a thirty-page document. Well, here's the bald truth: you're going to write a storyline anyway, only it will be the first draft of your book. That means you'll write several hundred pages, not just thirty, which means it'll take you much more than four months—perhaps a year, likely longer. And when it's done you'll realize how sprawling and unfocused the manuscript is, so you'll have to spend several more months fixing it. And that's just the *first* draft.

That is a draining process. And a discouraging one.

Even worse, because that first draft of the book took so long to write, you'll resist doing the extensive work necessary to rewrite it. You'll cling to mediocre material. Your choices about character and plot—which, after all, were just your first choices—will feel set in stone, so you'll try to chisel away at offending parts, when really you should knock down the whole thing to its core elements and start again.

Don't put yourself through that agony. Build a storyline instead. It will save you grief, and it will help you write a better book.

Planning Is Creativity

"The enemy of art is the absence of limitations."
– Orson Wells

Inexperienced writers often resist working on a storyline for fear it will inhibit their creativity. In fact, the opposite is true: writing a storyline is energizing and liberating. That's because in a storyline you can test concepts, try out notions, and if they don't prove robust, toss them away. You can be bold with plot ideas. You can change characters—add them, trash them, perhaps streamline two who serve a similar dramatic function into one (I've done that more than once)—all without facing the monumental task of rewriting the whole damn book.

> It's a vital artistic paradox. Total freedom inhibits creativity; strategic limits generate creativity.

Here's an example of this concept of strategic limits. If I say to you, "Write five pages about anything you want" you might tense up, floundering in that sea of vagueness, thinking: Where the hell do I begin? But if I say, "Write about one thing that made you belly-laugh as a child, one friend you envied as a teenager, and one time you saw your father cry," I guarantee those specifics would strike sparks in your mind and you would rush into writing. The imposed limits force creative ideas from the writer the way champagne shoots from its bottle.

John Cleese, the much admired British actor-comedian, made this very serious statement: "Creativity is not a talent. It's a way of operating."

Speaking of John Cleese's comedic art, there are striking parallels between the storylining process and the preparation process in many other arts. As an example, let's look at the field of acting. This is turf I know well, having made my living as an actor before I became an author. The rehearsal period for most professional acting companies is often just four weeks. (The exception is big Broadway-bound musical productions that can require months of rehearsal.) Four weeks isn't much time to get a play up "on the boards," yet the *last* thing an acting company does is enact the entire play. The process has to be broken down into workable stages.

Here's the usual rehearsal schedule. The first day is just for a read-through of the play by the whole cast sitting around a table with the director and stage manager. The remainder of the first week is spent on "blocking," the term used for working out just which characters move where, and when. That's all the actors do in week one. The next couple of weeks are dedicated to detailed scene development. Working in a rehearsal space that's usually just a large room (you're not on stage yet), the director works on individual scenes, often out of sequence, with just the handful of actors who appear in each scene, delving for motivation, nuance, and pacing. Not until the final week does the cast do run-throughs of the whole play, on stage, followed by technical rehearsals (sound cues and light cues) and finally the full dress rehearsal.

The point is that each phase of the rehearsal process is dedicated to specific tasks and goals. If, at the start, any acting company were so foolish as to plunge into simply running through the whole play over and over with full cast and all the tech effects, the result would be weeks of chaos with the final product a mess. The rehearsal process has to be done in manageable segments.

So it is with storylining. The goal is to gradually construct a coherent, satisfying plot that springs from character. Later, for your first full book-length draft, the goal is to enrich the story with complexity, nuance, and rhythm. In later book drafts, the goal is to polish and refine. You simply cannot do all these things at once. So, first you build your story in the storyline, taking weeks, often months, and only when you've finished your final draft of the storyline do you start writing the book-length work. Believe me, by then you're bursting to write it. The process, far from withering your creativity, vitalizes it and makes it bloom.

Here's the same principle applied to another art: sculpture. I once watched a sculptor give a public demonstration of creating a bust: a head in clay. I knew nothing about sculpting, so I was fascinated by his remarks to a group of us onlookers as he worked. He told us that the classic way students learn basic structure in sculpting clay is to build up the form, then note what's not right about it—maybe the nose is too long, the lips weak, the cheekbones not pronounced enough—then break it down, mash it back into a formless mass, then start to build it up again. Next time perhaps the nose is right, but now the lips are too full, and the cheekbones still need refining. So the sculptor breaks it down again, then builds it up again—over and over and over. I loved hearing him explain this, because I felt how startlingly similar the process is for a writer working on their storyline. You've got to build up your story design, then tear it apart and re-build it, over and over and over.

Now, do you want to do that with a four-hundred page manuscript or a thirty- page storyline?

Successful authors know this. Bestselling author John Grisham said in an interview: "The more time I spend on the outline, the easier it is to write the book." He added that outlining was a lesson he learned the hard way after writing his first novel, *A Time to Kill*. That manuscript was over nine hundred pages. "It was a mess," he said, and eventually he cut three hundred pages, a process that took "a lot of hard work." So when he wrote his next book, *The Firm*, he started with an outline. In other words, a storyline. *The Firm* became his first bestseller.

STORYLINE DRAFTS

"The work consists of pushing, pulling, prodding and otherwise trying to wrest a story from a glimmer of a notion."
—MARILYN WALLACE

No writer comes up with a wholly satisfying storyline on the first attempt. You'll do several storyline drafts. Best-selling novelist Joy Fielding says on her website: "I start with characters, a theme, a basic idea, then I write an outline. Often, it takes two or three outlines to get it right. Very often, I go way off track at the beginning."

So do I. It always takes me more than three drafts of a storyline to get it right. My process is to begin with a one-page or two-page concept, because usually at the outset I have only the broadest strokes of the story. That is, I have a main character and their problem—what their goal is, and why achieving it is a challenge because another character, an antagonist, presents obstacles. I also have a rough idea of one or more of the developments of their conflict, but, again, just broad strokes. Usually, when I begin my storyline, I have no idea yet of the story's climax.

Gradually, through several storyline drafts, I expand those couple of pages, enriching the pivotal characters, introducing catalyst characters, testing several turning points, refining ideas, and working out a climax. During this whole period I'm also doing research, which inevitably sparks story ideas. Eventually, my storyline is about thirty pages, double-spaced, and has the story's beginning, middle, and end, charting all the main characters' significant actions. In other words, I have the backbone of the entire plot.

Once you have that backbone you'll be ready to begin writing your book's first full draft. As mystery author George C. Chesboro puts it, "I will begin my first draft when my plot outline has become a kind of map, however rough, that will at least get me from one end of the land of my story to the other; I know the terrain at the beginning of my journey, the landscape at the end, and have some idea of the mountains I must cross, the rivers I must ford, in between."

Plot and characters can and do change, often significantly, from your storyline to your book-length first draft. That's normal; no storyline details are written in stone. But all the heavy lifting of story design is done when your storyline is done. The time it takes will save you anguish later on.

When you take the care to work up a storyline, you'll create vital active characters and a robust plot that will only grow stronger when you write the book.

Seven Tips for Storylining

Tip #1. Write your storyline in the present tense, even if your novel will be written in the past tense. This isn't a "rule," merely a suggestion. The reason is that the present tense keeps the action feeling immediate, as though it's happening *now*. (See the excerpt of my storyline for *The Queen's Exiles* at the end of this chapter.)

Tip #2. Write a paragraph or so about each main character as they enter the story: their central goal, their motivation, and a little backstory.

Tip #3. Write a paragraph or so about the central action of each major scene: the characters' specific goals in the scene, the scene's conflict, and the scene's outcome.

Tip #4. Don't get bogged down in details of dialogue, description, setting, backstory, or interior monologues. A storyline shouldn't be a mini-novel. It's a document of just what *happens*.

For example, regarding dialogue, keep *direct* dialogue out of your storyline. The reason is that we all fall in love with the dialogue we write because it's so alive and such a pleasure to create. But that doesn't necessarily make your first renderings the most effective. By the time you write your first book-length draft you will likely have refined much about the characters, making them subtly (or even radically) different than in your first storyline draft, so you will need to adjust their dialogue accordingly, but you'll itch to preserve the dialogue you fell in love with. Instead, I recommend that you stick to economically *indirect* dialogue so you don't become fixated on the character's actual words. (Example of direct dialogue: Colin tells Amy, "I confessed to the captain. I told him that yes, bloody right I did it!" Example of indirect dialogue: Colin boldly tells Amy that he confessed his crime to the captain.) However, even with indirect dialogue, limit yourself to just the crucial dialogue exchanges that move the plot forward: no chit-chat. The example above (a character confessing to a crime) moves the plot forward, whereas *Colin tells Amy he likes her dress* likely does not.

Tip # 5. Maintain separate files for notes about the myriad enriching details of character, setting, and backstory, and even some zinger lines of dialogue. You'll have dozens, even hundreds of thoughts about these constantly popping into your head, so do save them in files of their own. It will be necessary to sift through them later and use many of them in your novel, but not in your storyline. For the storyline, bear in the mind the KISS mantra: "Keep it simple, stupid." A storyline is for just broad strokes.

Tip #6. Construct your storyline by identifying and focusing on the story's plot points. These are reversals the characters experience. A reversal is an unexpected consequence of their actions. In other words, the character takes an action to try to get what they want, but faces an outcome that's different. Successful novels contain many reversals, small and large. A *major* reversal is called a turning point. If you construct your storyline in three acts (and I recommend that you do) you will have a turning point as the climax of Act One, another as the climax of Act Two, and another as the climax of Act Three, which is also the story climax. (See more about reversals and turning points in Chapter 5.)

Tip #7. Expect your first complete storyline draft to be somewhat poorly focused, with clichés of character and some unresolved plot strands. Don't worry; you'll freshen and resolve these things in the next drafts. There will be shortcomings in each full draft of the novel too. All that matters is the *final* draft. That takes time. Remember—it's a process.

It can be helpful for you to see a storyline that led to a published book, so at the end of this chapter you can read part of a storyline draft for my novel *The Queen's Exiles*.

The Research Lode

While you're working on your storyline you'll also be doing research. Each step feeds the other. The struggle to create characters and build a plot sends you to do research, and the research, in turn, sparks ideas for characters and plot. It's a symbiotic process that moves forward organically.

All writers do research, because it's essential to know the worlds of your characters. Whether you're writing about a divorce lawyer, a medieval musician, a fighter pilot, or a kindergarten teacher, your depiction of their daily life and activities must be based on reality. Find out about that reality by reading everything you can, in fiction and non-fiction, about their world. Also, interview anyone in that field who will talk to you. For example, if you're writing a scene in a hospital emergency room, and you have a brother-in-law whose cousin is an ER nurse, talk to her. A source like that will give you facts that are more specific and more vivid than anything you could invent.

An extraordinary detail was told to me when I was researching my thriller *Beyond Recall* (published by Warner Books under my penname Stephen Kyle). The central character is a physician with Doctors Without Borders, and an episode takes place in Rwanda during that country's nightmarish genocidal war in the 1980s. I contacted Doctors Without Borders and spoke to its then director, Doctor James Orbinski, who had treated wounded people in Rwanda during the worst of the wartime atrocities. He kindly agreed to an interview, and we met over breakfast in a deli-style Toronto restaurant. I brought my list of questions, and he told me the following chilling detail.

At a rural village, he said, there was a little churchyard where people who had been attacked by a machete-wielding mob were straggling in from all over: men and women with missing limbs; children with horrific wounds. There wasn't nearly enough room or staff to treat them all, so the nurses had to do a difficult triage. They moved through this courtyard of misery and taped a number to each patient's forehead. The people had no idea what the numbers meant, but the doctors did. A number "1" meant the patient must be seen immediately. A "2" meant the patient could wait a bit. A "3" meant leave them to die. Did I use that heartrending detail in my book? Absolutely.

To get authentic, vivid details for my novels I've interviewed all sorts of people: a Brazilian mine owner, a tropical disease expert, a criminal lawyer, a priest, a sheep farmer, and an ambassador, to name a few. In *The Experiment* my protagonist is a movie stuntwoman, so I interviewed a couple. But interviews don't have to be face-to-face; often a phone call will get you all the information you need.

Sometimes you'll find experts close to home. Writing my first historical novel, I discovered an eye-opening resource: the man I married. *The Queen's Lady* is set in England during the reign of Henry VIII, and although my husband shares no similarities with

Henry regarding tyrannical rule and beheaded wives—I married a thoughtful, peaceable man—he is endowed with the standard issue male anatomy, and this helped my research. Here's how. In my first draft I'd written a scene of a Midsummer Eve celebration in which boisterous revelers dance around bonfires, lovers steal kisses, and a drunk old man pisses as he staggers through the crowd.

Wait a minute, I thought: can a man do that, urinate while walking? I took the problem to my husband. "Can a man do that?" I asked.

"I'll go see," he said, and walked out the door.

Thankfully, we lived at the time on sixty rural acres, not a soul around. A few minutes later he came back in.

"Yup," he reported.

You can see why I value this resource.

Seriously, don't be shy about asking for information. When I began writing years ago and I contacted people to request an interview, I was afraid they'd be annoyed and would turn me down, especially if they were busy professionals. But their response was the opposite. I found that people *love* to talk about their work; they're proud of what they do. Furthermore, experts in their field like to know that you're going to get the facts right. Just make sure you're well prepared when you approach them; busy people don't want to chit-chat. Assure them, when you contact them, that you'll take just fifteen or twenty minutes of their time and will have a prepared list of questions. Your expert will relax and be glad to tell you what you need.

It's also helpful to visit, if possible, the locations where your story takes place, in order to get precise and accurate details about settings. This applies not just to writers of contemporary novels but also to historical novelists, for although much about the locales may have changed over the centuries, you can still get a "feel" for a place by walking in the footsteps of the characters in your book and taking notes. (The exception, of course, is if you're writing fantasy or science fiction; for that, you'll be doing your own world-building.) Take photos, too, when you visit your book's locations. When I was planning *The Experiment*, which is set mostly in New York City, I planned for my heroine to live aboard a small sailboat there, so I visited a marina on City Island in the Bronx and took pictures. One was of an old-fashioned bridge. I'd taken it at random, but once home at my desk and flipping through the photos, I realized that the bridge would be the ideal spot for my mid-story chase sequence.

If you can't get to the locations in your story, don't worry. You'll glean valuable details by reading books, both fiction and non-fiction, set in the same or similar locales, and you'll find plenty of material online, including photos. My thriller *After Shock* is set in Alaska, so I spent many hours studying pictures and poring through books about Alaska's bush pilots, prospectors, politicians, and plain folks, and when the novel was released I received mail from readers who praised its authenticity and said they felt they were "right there." Yet I'd never gone to Alaska.

Do lots of research so that you can write accurately about the world your characters live in, but don't let the research process so enthrall you it brings your writing to a halt. I often do what I call "just-in-time" research: I'll sketch in some less-than-perfect facts about a particular situation as I write the novel's first draft, because I don't want to hamper the writing momentum by spending hours online or days interviewing people. Then, before I write the second draft I'll nail down the facts, finding out everything I need to be accurate.

Also, don't let your fascination in the research lead you to insert long, moribund passages of background information, what editors call "info dumps," that drag down your story's pace. Research shouldn't draw attention to itself. The goal is to distill the facts so that they unobtrusively illuminate the life of your novel. One writer said this about doing research: "It's like making mashed potatoes: you've got to get rid of the lumps."

Book Drafts

You've now done your research and finished your storyline and are prepared to write your novel. You'll know when you're ready. You'll have a sense that it's time. Harking back to the words of mystery author George C. Chesboro, you'll now have the rough map of your story in hand. Prepared to start on the journey across its terrain, you're in a position to say: "I now know the mountains I must cross, the rivers I must ford."

Be aware that it's going to require several drafts. That's normal. Here's what legendary literary agent Albert Zuckerman, who has midwifed dozens of bestselling books, says in his own book *Writing the Blockbuster Novel*: "The likelihood of your novel being terrific in every respect the first time you set it down is from slight to nonexistent." Most successful authors write several drafts, and virtually all write at least three. My recommendation is to focus on a specific goal for each draft.

Think of each draft as a layer. Every layer adds complexity.

First Draft

There is one universally acknowledged truth about first drafts: they're always bad. That word "bad" is, of course, a subjective term in any context, but I'm referring specifically to the context of writing a compelling story, so here "bad" could mean the story is unfocused and rambling, or it might be fragmentary and unfinished, or it might be laden with clichés of both character and plot. Every writer's first draft suffers from weaknesses like these. So, your goal should be to get through the first draft as quickly as possible so that you can set to work improving its weaknesses. Don't be dismayed by the loose ends and holes and clichés and stiff dialogue. You're going to fix all those things in your next drafts. Just press on to the end. Remember, all that matters is the final draft.

Bestselling author Joy Fielding says: "I go way off track at the beginning. I've had to write the first halves of my novels many times before I got them right." She's far from alone. Authors make many changes from their first draft to their final draft. When Tennessee Williams wrote the first drafts of his play *A Streetcar Named Desire* he had Blanche Dubois headed for a happy ending. It's hard to imagine, given the tragic tone of this famous play, yet Williams wrote a number of scenes in which Blanche found a measure of love and redemption instead of ruin and insanity. Then he did a major revision.

So, I recommend that you get your first draft written quickly, then pause. And congratulate yourself. By finishing a first draft you've done what thousands say they want to but never do: you've written a whole novel.

But it's not that good yet. So, put the draft aside for a week or two. Do something else. Take a holiday if you can, or do some gardening, or paint the spare bedroom. Whatever, put the book aside. Then, after a week or two, take it out and look at it again with fresh eyes. Read it with all the objectivity you can muster. I like to visualize an actual reader, not a friend or relative but someone like the clerk at my bank, someone I've said "Hi" to for years but don't really know. I imagine her taking this book on vacation and I ask myself, would she find the story gripping and concise? I suggest that you read through the draft quickly, taking no notes. Don't let the potholes in the story bother you. Just let the story wash over you and affect you.

Now, do a second reading with pen and paper at hand and make notes on every pothole you encounter: every muddy action, every repetition, every boring passage, every unresolved plot strand. Be merciless in pinpointing the story's weaknesses.

Then, set about deciding how you're going to deal with them.

Further Drafts

Your copious notes will bring you to launching into your second draft. The good news is that this is the most enjoyable part of the work. You know your characters intimately now—they feel like living, breathing people. And you can see that you have a workable story, but perhaps it's obscured by extraneous material, or perhaps the opposite, not fully developed. Now is the time to fix it.

Your second draft is for cutting out deadwood detail, especially dormant masses of backstory and overgrown clumps of description. It's also your last chance to be bold. Cut a whole scene if it doesn't work. Change a character's motivation. Rebuild your climax to intensify the characters' emotions and actions. Enrich and sharpen every scene.

After that, you're ready to do your final draft. This draft is for polishing. This is where you pluck out the little burrs of clumsy dialogue. You tighten a scene's lagging pace. You refine any overwritten scene openings and endings—that is, a scene should start not with a timid tip-toeing into it but with something already underway, and should end not by trailing off with anti-climactic extra words but instead leave a question hovering. As screenwriters wisely say about scenes, "Get in late, and get out early." Also, this draft is where you work, finally and carefully, on word choice, cutting every superfluous word, finding fresh phrases to replace the clichés that have acted until now as place markers, and perfecting your metaphors and similes.

Finally, you've finished your third draft (or fifth, or whatever number it may be) and you think the book is pretty damn good. But don't trust just yourself. Don't trust friends or family either, unless they're professional writers or editors. Friends and relatives can usually offer only vague comments like, "I think it's great," or, if they're disappointed, "It was okay." Neither response will help you, because rarely are friends and family (I call them "civilians") able to articulate what works, dramatically, and what doesn't work. More important, they can't articulate *why* something doesn't work.

Returning to the example of an acting company rehearsing a play, the producer and director never allow members of the public (civilians) to watch rehearsals, and it's for the same reason. Such people, disappointed at seeing lags and holes in the show, have nothing constructive to contribute. They don't understand that the development of the product is a process—a painstaking, deliberate merging of disparate elements. The producer, director, cast, and crew know that all that matters is the result on opening night.

So, with your manuscript, it's wise now to get an expert reader to review it and offer specific suggestions about improving it. Established authors are fortunate because our publishers provide us with in-house editors who pore over our manuscripts and make detailed comments toward revision. In addition, many of us benefit from the fine editorial skills of our agents. But writers who don't yet have this kind of expert team need to find help elsewhere. So I recommend that you find a professional story editor, someone who has no reason to stroke your ego. Once you have solid editing suggestions from a pro, you'll be in an excellent position to do the final re-write of your book, and to make it the best it can be: a page-turner.

Example of a Storyline

It can be helpful for you to see an example of a storyline that led to the creation of a published book. What follows is an excerpt from a draft of the storyline I wrote for *The Queen's Exiles*, the sixth book in my series, The Thornleigh Saga. This excerpt covers about a third of the story.

**Storyline for *The Queen's Exiles*
by Barbara Kyle**

Act I

1572. The English Isle of Sark in the English Channel.

Fenella Doorn, thirty, Scottish by birth, watches a ship damaged by cannon fire limp into her bay. Fenella has built a successful, if unorthodox, enterprise salvaging vessels. These include some from the small fleet manned by Dutch rebels called the Sea Beggars who are fighting the brutal Spanish occupation of the Netherlands, a conflict from which Fenella herself is a refugee. For her the repair work is just business: she considers the resistance movement hopeless; imperial Spain is invincible. But she is intrigued by the crippled ship that's arriving. It's one she has heard about, captained by an English baron who has joined the Sea Beggars in their attacks on Spanish vessels.

Going aboard she finds that the baron-captain is Adam Thornleigh. Eleven years ago in Edinburgh, fleeing an abusive relationship, Fenella helped Adam break out of jail so she could escape with him on a boat. In their days at sea she fell in love with him, though he was so weak and sick from captivity he hardly seemed to notice her. They reached the Netherlands and parted, and Fenella started a new life. But she has never forgotten him.

Eleven years ago Adam definitely noticed Fenella, a woman both lovely and brave, and one to whom he owes his life. His crew now bring out Spanish prisoners—a half dozen common seamen and a nobleman—and prepare to hang them. Fenella recognizes the nobleman. She demands that the crew halt the hangings. She sends the seamen off to safety in a boat. Then she pulls out a pistol and shoots the nobleman.

Adam hears why. She married a Dutch shipbuilder, a good man who five years ago was killed in the massacre of their town ordered by the Spanish commander she just shot. Adam confides the extent of his involvement with the Dutch resistance. He is helping the Sea Beggars with the covert blessing of Queen Elizabeth, who has given the rebel ships safe haven in English ports, and he has done such damage to the Spanish that the Duke of Alba, who governs the Netherlands, has put a price on his head. Adam needs his ship repaired so he can resume the fight. Fenella sets her shore crew to the task. It will take weeks, so

Adam asks to buy a boat from her to sail to the Netherlands. He has a private mission to carry out before he returns for his ship.

Fenella knows her love for Adam is hopeless—he's a wealthy baron while she is utterly common; and he's married—but despite that she seizes a chance to be with him. When she came to Sark as a refugee she came with her late husband's father who is now very ill and has asked her to take him home to fight the Spaniards before he dies. She refused, pitying his obsession since he's so sick, and reluctant herself to go near the troubles in the Netherlands, but now she offers to sail him home and offers to take Adam with them.

On the voyage Adam confides to her his private mission. Three years ago his wife Frances collaborated in an attempt to kill Queen Elizabeth, then escaped, taking their young children Kate and Robert with her. Adam has been looking for them ever since, first in Ireland, then Spain, and now has had word from his Dutch agent that Frances and the children are in Brussels. He has nothing but contempt for his wife, but he is determined to get his children back. The voyage with Fenella has brought them close, and by the time they approach Antwerp, he is deeply in love with her. They anchor in a secluded bay, and Fenella dares to dream of a future with Adam.

They part to see to their business, she to take her sick father-in-law home to his village, Adam to track down his wife. They promise to rendezvous here on the boat in two weeks, hopefully with his children, and then return to Sark for his ship.

In Brussels, Carlos Valverde commands the Duke of Alba's militia keeping the peace. He and his wife Isabel are dining with Alba, a gracious host. Carlos's marriage has been a happy one, and Isabel is pregnant with their fourth child, but there is a strained discord between them. Even before they arrived in the Netherlands over a year ago Isabel was against Carlos taking this commission. He is adamant, however, that it was the right move. He made England his home after marrying Isabel Thornleigh, but their English estate has not brought profit, only debt, and although he has been loyal to Queen Elizabeth she never warmed to him because he is Spanish, so Carlos has not won the preferment in England he deserves. Carlos used to be a captain of cavalry who saw action all over Europe, and Alba was a general he once fought for, so when he heard that Alba was made governor of the Netherlands he requested the commission to command the Brussels militia.

In the city center he and Isabel make their way through the crowd at a mass execution of rebels. Isabel has always been appalled by Alba's brutal rule. She wants to go home; she does not want her baby born into this awful place. Carlos insists that he has to succeed here, and confesses that they are in far worse financial difficulty than he told her. Their debts are huge. With their family growing, he is determined to prove himself to Alba in the hope of securing a pension from Philip of Spain. He tells Isabel he wants her to stay, but if he has to remain here alone, he will.

Fenella takes her father-in-law to his home village where they hear shocking news. Fenella's husband, Claes Doorn, is alive. He survived the town massacre five years ago and became a rebel, working underground. The Duke of Alba has issued a death warrant against him. Claes is in hiding.

Act II
Adam's wife Frances, Baroness Thornleigh, meets his agent whom she is paying to keep her informed. With this knowledge

she has been able to outrun Adam. But Frances hates her exile, constantly hiding and moving to keep one step ahead of Adam. She longs to go home but cannot as long as Elizabeth is queen. If she were to set foot in England she would hang. The agent tells her that Adam has reached Antwerp to track her down, and that he came with a woman.

Frances is frightened about Adam finding her, but she has an ally in the Duke of Alba. She and her hostess, the Countess of Feria, along with others members of the exiled Catholic English nobility, are planning to overthrow Elizabeth and put Mary, Queen of Scots on the throne, and they want Spain to back them. Frances is in contact with Mary. They ask Alba to support the English coup, and he promises to recommended the plan to King Philip.

Frances is at the countess's house when Adam confronts her. She pleads with him for a reconciliation, saying that if he will persuade Elizabeth to pardon her they can put the past behind them and live again as man and wife. He tells her she's insane; she's lucky he doesn't drag her home to hang. He demands that she surrender Kate and Robert. She says they are not with her, and she won't divulge their whereabouts.

Alba arrives to discuss the planned English coup. Adam barely escapes.

Frances tells Alba that Adam has found her. Alba sends soldiers after him, but they lose him. Alba tells Frances to send him word if she learns where Adam can be found and captured.

Fenella reaches the rebel group in hiding led by her husband Claes. He is overjoyed to see her, for he believed, as she did of him, that she died five years ago in the town slaughter. Overwhelmed and confused, Fenella is sure of only one thing: Claes must leave the country before Alba finds him and hangs him. She offers to smuggle him out on her boat. But Claes refuses. He tells her he is committed to driving out the Spanish, and will fight them until they leave or he is dead. He asks her to stay with him and join him in the fight.

Adam confronts his turncoat agent leaving Frances's house. Under Adam's ungentle questioning the agent reveals that Kate and Robert are in a convent. Adam reaches the convent but finds that Frances has posted guards to keep him from the children. He gets a message in to Kate. She and Robert sneak out and meet him. It's a happy reunion for Adam and his daughter, but Robert is reticent—Frances has poisoned his mind about his father. Adam knows he needs help to get his children out. He promises them he'll be back to take them home.

Fenella makes the rendezvous with Adam on her boat. She has made the hard decision that her place is with Claes, but she cannot mention him for fear of putting him and his fellow rebels in danger. Her heart is breaking as she pretends coldness to Adam, telling him she has met another man and is staying to be with him. Adam, shocked and hurt, says she has reverted to her true self as the whore she was when he first met her. Wounded, Fenella orders him off her boat. They part in acrimony.

Returning to Claes's house, Fenella sees a troop of Alba's men surround the house. She hides and witnesses the soldiers capturing Claes and his fellow rebels, and sees that the soldiers' commander is Carlos Valverde. Back in Scotland Carlos defended her from the abusive garrison commander she was living with, then helped her and Adam escape. Powerless to save Claes, Fenella watches Carlos take him and his friends away to Alba's prison to face certain death.

Adam, bitter about Fenella, goes to his sister Isabel for help in getting his children. It's a risk, since her husband Carlos could hand him over to Alba, but Adam is trusting in the strength of family bonds. Face to face with his brother–in–law, though, he can't hide his contempt for the work Carlos is doing—Alba's dirty work. Carlos makes no apology for keeping the peace for the lawful governor. Adam curbs his hostility: he needs Carlos. He explains that Frances has the children under guard in the convent and asks Carlos to help him get them out. Isabel urges Carlos to help rescue their niece and nephew.

Adam and Carlos reach the convent and overcome the guards and get the children out. Mission accomplished, Carlos leaves; he would lose his post, maybe his life, if Alba found he had helped the "English pirate." Adam is alone with the children when assassins come after him. He's sure Alba hired them. Fearing that Kate and Robert will be taken by the assassins, he tells the children to run back to the convent, then leads the killers after him. His only hope is to reach the sea. He takes Fenella's boat.

Fenella sees a mass hanging of Claes's friends. Sickened by the deaths, she knows that Claes, in jail, is awaiting his own execution day at which Alba intends to make a gruesome spectacle of him as a warning to other dissidents. Fenella decides there is only way to save Claes and stop Alba's reign of terror. She must kill Alba.

She visits Carlos's house. Meeting Isabel, she says she has come to thank Carlos for helping her in Scotland. Alone with Carlos she pretends to break down, telling him she is penniless and has come to ask him to take her to Alba. She explains that she and the general enjoyed a brief tryst many years ago when she was very young and needed money. Alba always fancied her and may now make her his mistress, which would save her from penury. Carlos, sympathetic, agrees to take her to Alba's palace. When Fenella has gone, Isabel questions Carlos about her. He is silent about Fenella's situation, adding more stress to his already tense marriage.

At Alba's palace Fenella contrives to get close to Alba and pulls a pistol to shoot him. Horrified, Carlos stops her and disarms her. Alba has Fenella arrested ...

Note: The above storyline excerpt covers about a third of the story. This was an early storyline draft, and the published novel differs in several key scenes.

Another tool I have devised is a step-outline. There is no "rule" that says you must work up such a document, but I find it invaluable because it lays out in small bites the narrative's essential actions. A step-outline is not rendered in narrative form the way a storyline is; rather, it's a shorthand list of the action in each scene. I prepare it to keep me focused on just *what happens*, and I do this by limiting each scene to a single line. That's often a challenge, but worth the effort, because by ruthlessly paring down the book to its bare-bones actions I get a feel for its pace and rhythm.

I revise and update the step-outline as I work through drafts of the storyline and of the full novel, so it's not completely finished until the book itself is finished. I tape the step-outline on the wall beside my computer, replacing it often with revised updates, glancing at it often to keep me focused on the through lines.

Note: The numbers indicate chapter numbers. Scenes within a chapter are divided by a slash. The character's name in boldface is the POV character.

Step-Outline for *The Queen's Exiles*

1

Fenella greets Adam, saves captive Spanish seamen, shoots Don Alfonso

2

Adam hears from Johan about Fenella / makes plan to find Frances and get his children

Fenella rejects Adam's offer to resettle in England, says she'll go to Antwerp for her gold

3

Carlos captures vandal/is denied pension & told by Alba to find Adam/argues with Isabel

4

Fenella arranges to get her gold / takes Johan home / is captured by rebels, sees Claes

Act II

5

Frances hears Adam is coming / asks Alba for aid vs. Eliz, is asked by Alba to find Adam

6

Fenella hears Claes will ambush Spanish, she offers to take money to the Brethren

7

Adam plans with Tyrone / begs Kate to leave, sees Frances send in soldiers, fights, escapes

8

Fenella reaches Berck's boat / sees Adam arrive wounded / nurses him

9

Carlos & Isabel are confronted by Frances, they argue / are faced with Adam asking help

10

Carlos clears the convent for Adam

Adam awaits Kate&Robert, gets them on horseback, is shot at, must leave them, escapes

11

Fenella meets Mme B / sees Carlos's troop bring prisoners to hang incl. Johan & Claes

12

Fenella sees Johan hang, sees Claes taken away, hears he's being saved for execution

Adam waits for Fenella / is attacked, kills assassin/gets Fenella's message: she's staying

13

Adam reaches Sark, finds ship burned / rejoins Beggars, asks for guns, LaM demands raid

14

Fenella follows Carlos home to enable her plan to kill Alba, follows him into stable

Carlos tells Isabel he'll get pension, sees her disapproval of raid

Fenella asks Carlos for intro, he won't, she begs Isabel who tells Carlos to help F

15

Adam raids/Beggars get expelled/persuades LaM to attack with Brethren/reaches cove

16

Fenella approaches Alba at brothel, pulls pistol to shoot, Carlos disarms & arrests her …

This step-outline excerpt, as with the storyline excerpt, covers about a third of the story. You'll see that, from the storyline to the step-outline, I made some story refinements. Nothing is written in stone. Remember, all that matters is the novel's final draft, the one you're ultimately ready to submit to an agent or publisher.

CHAPTER 5

ESSENTIALS OF STORY STRUCTURE

"Tell the reader a story! Because without a story,
you are merely using words to prove you can
string them together in logical sentences."
ANNE MCCAFFREY

O f all the arts, writing may be the most deceptive, because in our culture virtually everyone can read and everyone can write: letters, emails, business reports. This leads people to assume that a novel is just a longer version of such documents, since it uses the same components of words, sentences, and paragraphs. Unlike other arts. Painting, for example. Though we can all draw stick figures, we know we couldn't possibly create a portrait until we'd learned basic techniques like proportion and perspective and how to wield paint. Or music. No one would dream of trying to compose symphonic music until they'd mastered music notation, music theory, and had spent years playing at least one instrument, likely more. Yet many people believe that to write a novel you just sit down and the art flows. It doesn't. A novel does not tumble, fully formed, out of the writer's mind.

> Creating a tight, engaging story takes planning and design. And to design effectively, you need a knowledge of story structure.

THREE-ACT STRUCTURE

From the beginning of human society, stories have been told in three parts: an inciting incident, complications, and climax. In our time, thanks to centuries of theater and, more recently, film, this has become known as three-act structure. I believe that three-act structure is how our brains understand story: beginning, middle, end. And I believe that story is how we understand life. We comprehend each event we experience as having a beginning, a middle, and an end.

This goes very deep. Many experiences we value most, or consider the most profound, occur in three acts. People meet, fall in love, get married. Enemies confront each other, fight, then win or lose. A journey is three acts: you set out, you travel, you arrive. A meal is three acts: appetizer, main course, dessert. Lovemaking? Foreplay, intercourse, climax. The scientific method has three acts: hypothesis, experiment, proof. So does an essay: thesis, development, conclusion. We measure time in three stages:

past, present, future. And we measure our very time on earth in three acts: birth, life, death.

Three is a magical number that occurs over and over in myths and fairy tales, and it carries magic because sensing three parts to every experience is how we understand our lives: beginning, middle, end. So, in story, which is a metaphor for life, three-act structure is fundamental. Inciting incident. Complications. Climax.

If you've ever told a joke you already know the bare bones of story structure. In fact, every child knows it.

> "Knock-knock."
> "Who's there?"
> "Ach."
> "Ach who?"
> "Bless you!"

That little drama fulfills the basic requirements of a story: an inciting incident (knock, knock), complications ("Who's there?" "Ach" "Ach who?") and a climax that's a small revelation. From earliest childhood and on into adulthood, your brain will have absorbed this essence of story structure from reading stories, hearing stories, and watching stories on screen.

However, *responding* to a story is very different from knowing how to *create* a story. Even among academics and literary critics who can expertly parse story structure, few are able to translate that keen observational skill into an innovative skill: creating something from nothing. Since you're reading this book, your hunger to master the craft suggests that you have the creative skill, so you're likely already using some components of effective story structure in your writing, doing it by instinct. Some people's instincts for this are finely tuned, and that's what we call "talent."

Your instincts and talent, however, will supply only about half of what's needed in the writing process. Most people stop there. But for the many times when instinct falls short and talent gets stuck, structural analysis shows you how to get moving. If something you've written seems flat and lifeless, or poorly focused, and you wonder how to fix it, you go through your checklist of structural components. Is my inciting incident powerful enough to make my protagonist take action? Have I built this scene around a reversal? Does the climax bring my characters into direct confrontation? And so on. The parameters of story structure guide you. Again, it's that fascinating artistic paradox at play: total freedom inhibits creativity, whereas strategic limits generate creativity.

Sound story structure features these six essential major components:

1. The Hook
2. The Inciting Incident
3. The Overarching Story Question
4. Reversals
5. Turning Points
6. The Climax

Let me here make an important distinction between "story structure" and "plot." Many emerging writers believe these terms are interchangeable, virtually identical. They are not.

The elements of story structure apply to *all* stories, while plot refers to each *unique* story. That is, every well-constructed story will be made up of the six elements above, which are immutable (rather like the "laws" of nature), but the plot of every story is new and unique, because it springs from its specific cast of people, evolving from what these individuals want and what they do to try to get it.

To put it another way, every satisfying story, whatever its plot, even a wildly original plot, can be overlaid by the fixed template of story structure, but, conversely, no quantity of strung-together actions, however intriguing the characters involved, can save a narrative that does not observe the fundamentals of story structure; for example, the lack of a climax. The distinction is important, because it's helpful for you to keep in mind this supremacy of story structure.

> Only by observing the immutable "physics" of story structure can you tap into your characters' unique motivations, desires, problems, and actions that will lead to the creation of your particular story's fresh and original plot.

1. THE HOOK

As writers, our first goal is to attach the reader to the page—that is, to create in them the desire to read on. So no matter how you choose to begin your novel, you need to craft an opening that hooks the reader.

> A hook is a novel's first sentence or first paragraph, and it functions as a promise to the reader, an unspoken assurance that some plateau of excitement lies ahead.

This is often done by posing a problem the main character is encountering, or by foreshadowing some problem they *will* encounter, or by simply establishing a unique character who snatches our attention. A good hook will also establish the book's tone and reflect some facet of its theme.

A hook can be barbed: an implement of capture. Or it can be smooth: a friendly arm wrapped around your elbow. What all hooks do is tug you.

Examples of Hooks

The first sentence of Herman Melville's *Moby-Dick* is: "Call me Ishmael." It's a famous line, and for good reason. First, it's what's called an imperative sentence; it says "Do this"—a command—so in those three words the speaker establishes an extraordinarily confident voice. Second, it gives us a name. Names have force. They conjure up a real flesh-and-blood person in the reader's mind. Third, that particular name, Ishmael, resonates with the Biblical character of the same name, the exiled first son of Abraham, and thus establishes a portentous theme. Pretty powerful stuff in just three simple words.

Look at the equally famous opening sentence of Charles Dickens's classic, *A Tale of Two Cities*: "It was the best of times, it was the worst of times ... " This is actually just the beginning of a very long sentence that repeats the intriguing parallel structure of opposites ("It was the best of times, it was the worst of times; it was the age of wisdom, it was the age of foolishness; it was the epoch of belief, it was the epoch of incredulity... " and so on). The tension in this opening sets up the reader emotionally for a complex, highly dramatic story.

Jane Austen's much-loved novel *Pride and Prejudice* begins with: "It is a truth universally acknowledged that a single man in possession of a good fortune must be in want of a wife." No one reading or hearing that sentence can withhold a small, wry smile. Which was precisely Austen's intent. She is telling you two basic things. First, this story is going to have a foundation of gentle humor. Second, it's going to be about love and marriage: it's a romance.

My novel *Beyond Recall* (published by Warner Books under my penname Stephen Kyle) begins with these two brief sentences: "The deadline was up. She would have to kill." This tells the reader two things: the stakes are life and death, and the character referred to is ruthless. This hook establishes tone: the reader immediately senses they're in thriller territory.

My historical novel *The Queen's Lady* begins with: "She would remember this forever after as the night she watched two men die, one at peace and one in terror." The reader is now poised to see these two deaths happen, and, again, the hook establishes tone.

Hook Techniques

There are many ways to wield this essential tool of writing craft. Here are some of the most effective:

1. Name a character.

As noted above with "Call me Ishmael," the opening sentence of *Moby-Dick,* names have a kind of magic. They carry power, because they conjure up a living, breathing person.

2. Raise a question in the reader's mind.

Toni Morrison starts her novel *Paradise* with these six, arresting words: "They shoot the white girl first." Instantly, the reader's mind lurches to ask: Who are "they"? Who's the girl? Why have they shot her?

3. Plunge straight into the plot.

Paul Auster's *City Of Glass* begins with: "It was a wrong number that started it, the telephone ringing three times in the dead of night, and the voice on the other end asking for someone he was not."

4. Foreshadow an intriguing element of plot.

Here's the opening sentence of Dick Francis's mystery *Straight*: "I inherited my brother's desk, his business, his gadgets, his enemies, his horses and his mistress. I inherited my brother's life, and it nearly killed me."

5. Show a character's personality quirk.

The opening of Vladimir Nabokov's ground-breaking *Lolita* tosses a small bombshell of Humbert Humbert's quirkiness: "Lolita, light of my life, fire of my loins. My sin, my soul. Lo-lee-ta: the tip of the tongue taking a trip of three steps down the palate to tap, at three, on the teeth. Lo. Lee. Ta."

6. Show a character's attitude.

Ford Maddox Ford begins *The Good Soldier* with the following statement: "This is the saddest story I ever heard." Right away we sense this narrator's attitude of world-weary dejection. (Plus, we're waiting now to hear what the "saddest" story is.) In J. D. Salinger's *The Catcher In The Rye,* the cocky attitude of teenage narrator Holden Caulfield is on full-frontal display in its first sentence: "If you really want to hear about it, the first thing you'll probably want to know is where I was born, and what my lousy childhood was like, and how my parents were occupied and all before they had me, and all that David Copperfield kind of crap, but I don't feel like going into it, if you want to know the truth."

7. Render a mysterious or suspenseful event.

George Orwell's novel *Nineteen-Eighty-Four* starts with: "It was a bright cold day in April and the clocks were striking thirteen."

8. Start at the story's climax.

Donna Tartt uses this technique to open her Pulitzer prize-winning novel *The Goldfinch.* Theo Decker is hiding out in an Amsterdam hotel room, where, as he says: "I'd been shut up for more than a week, afraid to telephone anybody or go out, and my heart scrambled and floundered at even the most innocent noises: elevator bell, rattle of the minibar cart, even church clocks tolling the hour." Having established Theo's crisis with a couple of pages of this situation, the author then loops back to the chronological start of Theo's story several years earlier, when he was thirteen.

Use any of these techniques and you'll have your reader intrigued, maybe even slightly on edge. In other words, happily hooked.

2. The Inciting Incident

In the Bruce Springsteen song *Dancing in the Dark* there's this lyric: "You can't start a fire without a spark." In any novel there must be an event that sparks the story to life. This is what's called the inciting incident.

Deciding where to start rolling out your story is crucial. It's also difficult. New writers often begin with paragraphs—sometimes pages—of description about places and characters, or with backstory (events in a character's life up to the moment the story begins). It's as if the writer, having diligently worked out these many complex details herself, can't wait to share them. But readers don't come to a book for details, they come to see people in action.

That's why the phrase "inciting incident" is a helpful one for the writer, because it suggests that necessary spark: something occurs that *incites* the protagonist to *do* something. The phrase itself implies action, so writers can't fool themselves into thinking that description or backstory constitute an inciting incident. Here's a helpful definition:

> The inciting incident is the event that throws your protagonist's world out of balance. The actions this character takes to try to regain balance form the story.

Two thousand years ago, the Roman poet Horace wrote that an epic poem should begin *in medias res*, which is Latin for "in the midst of things." He meant that a story should start by plunging into an already crucial situation, one that's part of a chain of events. Backstory—that is, exposition about the events that led up to this crucial moment—can then be woven in as the narrative goes forward. That was good advice when Horace wrote it two millennia ago and it's good advice still. Whether you're writing a mystery, a romance, a thriller, a fantasy, or a mainstream novel, introduce your protagonist when something vital is already at stake.

It doesn't have to be world-hanging-in-the-balance stakes, but it does have to seem like that to the character. For example, in Chapter Three I referred to the opening pages of Maeve Binchy's novel *Scarlet Feather*. They show Cathy Scarlet *in medias res*—in the middle of things. She has just opened a catering business and desperately wants to make a success of it, and she is on her way to cater the New Year's Eve party for her wealthy and powerful mother-in-law, who looks down on Cathy, the daughter of her maid. Cathy is well aware of what she's up against: her mother-in-law's antagonism can break her. So, success this night is vital to Cathy. High stakes.

Let me emphasize the importance of the inciting incident being an event that incites the protagonist to take *action*. Here's an example to illustrate what that means. *High Noon* is an acclaimed Western film of 1952, its screenplay written by Carl Foreman. Gary Cooper, who won an Academy Award for his performance, stars as Will Kane, marshal of a town whose people prove too cowardly to help him when he's faced with an old enemy coming to kill him. An inexperienced screenwriter might have written that film script to open with various shots of the town and its individual inhabitants—the barber shaving a customer, the blacksmith shoeing a horse, a woman buying flour at the general store, a bartender pouring whisky—believing these images will be effective because they set the scene and introduce the characters. But, in fact, shots like that would have little effect on a viewer. Why? Because virtually nothing is happening.

Instead, *High Noon* starts with three tough-looking men on horseback meeting outside the town, then riding toward it. There's no dialogue, so their mission is a mystery, but their grim faces portend danger. *Then* we get the shots of the various townspeople as tense word spreads that these outlaws are on their way, and each person reacts with astonishment, incredulity, or fear. This culminates in a scene of Marshal Kane, who's getting married and about to leave on his honeymoon, hearing what's afoot, that a man he'd once sent to prison, Frank Miller, is returning on the noon train to exact his revenge. Miller and his outlaw friends are coming for Kane. The point is that something ominous is immediately set in motion—the three tough men riding toward town—so the tension of the townspeople, and then of the marshal, grips the viewer.

In a novel, an opening that gives merely neutral descriptions of places and characters and characters' backstory is the equivalent of a film script opening with a string of neutral shots *before* anything has been set in motion, and would suffer from the same weakness: nothing is happening.

> Readers cannot feel involved with a character until they see them in action.

Action is the key. And the actions a character takes propel them into some form of conflict. Remember: conflict does not mean combat; it simply means problems. What problems does this person face in trying to achieve a goal? A character who has no problems, no obstacles to overcome, is a boring character and cannot drive a story forward. Nothing moves forward in a story except through conflict. Here's a recap of this principle:

> A compelling novel is built on situations that put increasing pressures on characters, forcing them to face more and more difficult challenges, so that they must make increasingly risky choices, leading them to take actions that eventually reveal their true natures.

This holds as true for Elizabeth Bennett in Jane Austen's *Pride and Prejudice* as for a hero in a Stephen King thriller.

So, what kind of event constitutes an inciting incident? A person's life can be horribly unbalanced by a murder, or a call to war, or getting fired. But the event doesn't have to be a negative one. Someone's world can be upset by winning the lottery. Or getting married. Or going on a date that changes their life.

Shakespeare's most powerful plays start with dynamic inciting incidents. In *Macbeth*, after two very brief scenes (the witches' introductory scene is a mere thirteen lines), Scene 3 brings on Macbeth. He has just won a great battle for his king, and he and his friend Banquo are riding across the heath when they come upon the three witches, who tell him that one day Macbeth *himself* will be king. Their prophecy stuns Macbeth—it upsets the balance in his life by inciting his ambition. How he strives to make the prophecy a reality is what the play is about.

In *Hamlet* the inciting incident occurs in Scene 5 when Hamlet is astounded at seeing the ghost of his father, who speaks to him. His father tells him he was murdered, poisoned by his own brother, Hamlet's Uncle Claudius. This extraordinary event instantly upsets the balance of Hamlet's life, inciting his desire for revenge. His quest to avenge his father is what the play is about.

In *King Lear*, Shakespeare's greatest tragedy, the inciting incident happens in the very first scene. Lear has called together his whole court to make an announcement. Everyone important is there, including Lear's three grown daughters and the visiting King of France and Duke of Burgundy, suitors of the youngest one. Lear grandly announces that he is stepping down. He's going to relinquish his crown, and intends to divide up his kingdom equally among his three daughters. All they have to do, he tells them, is to proclaim here in front of everyone how much they love him. Immediately, his two elder daughters give enthusiastic speeches, saying he's the best father in the world and they love him "more than word can wield the matter." Lear is highly gratified. Then he turns to his youngest daughter, his favorite daughter, Cordelia.

But she can't do it. She says: "Unhappy that I am, I cannot heave / my heart into my mouth. I love your Majesty / according to my bond, no more nor less / … Why have my sisters husbands if they say / they love you all? Haply, when I shall wed, / that lord whose hand doth take my plight shall carry / half my love with him, half my care and duty. / Sure, I shall never marry like my sisters / to love my father all."

This enrages Lear—that Cordelia would talk back to him in front of the whole court. In a fit of fury he disowns her and banishes her. Cordelia's refusal is the event that upsets the balance of Lear's life, inciting his rage. And from that terrible moment, the play hurtles on to its tragic conclusion in which Lear finally sees how wrong he has been about everyone.

Notice, too, how these plays start *in medias res*, in the middle of things. Here's what Lajos Egri says in his book *The Art of Dramatic Writing*: "Hamlet did not start when the curtain went up. Far from it. A murder had been committed before ... This play opens, then, not in the beginning but in the middle, after a dastardly act had been committed ... In fact, your story is only possible because it grew out of the very thing that happened before. It is imperative that your story starts in the middle, and not under any circumstances at the beginning."

Examples In Our Own Time

Shakespeare, of course, is always inspiring, but let's examine this concept of the inciting incident as used by writers closer to our own time. Look at the inciting incidents in two classic, 20th-century novels, both made into classic movies: L. Frank Baum's fantasy *The Wizard of Oz* and *Gone With the Wind,* Margaret Mitchell's Civil War saga.

The Wizard of Oz begins with Dorothy living a normal life on her aunt and uncle's farm—a boring life, in her eyes—when a tornado strikes and sweeps her up into the sky. The tornado is the inciting incident, radically upsetting the balance of Dorothy's life. It incites her desire, her need, to get back home, and from the moment she arrives in the magical world of Oz she takes action to try to accomplish this by setting out on the Yellow Brick Road.

Gone With the Wind begins with sixteen-year-old Scarlett O'Hara madly in love with Ashley Wilkes, so when she hears the news that Ashley intends to marry Melanie Hamilton, she is appalled. This incident so upsets the balance of Scarlett's life, she boldly declares her love to Ashley's face. He gently rebuffs her, and when Ashley and Melanie's wedding is hastened by the outbreak of war, Scarlett's heartbreak incites her to take a reckless action to keep Ashley in her life: she marries Melanie's brother Charles.

Coming into the 21st-century, note the inciting incidents that kick start two mega-bestselling novels: Gillian Flynn's noir thriller *Gone Girl* and Donna Tartt's Pulitzer Prize-winning *The Goldfinch*. In *Gone Girl* Nick Dunne discovers, on the morning of his fifth wedding anniversary, that his wife Amy has gone missing. This upsets the balance of his life, and his goal is to find her. He takes action by going to the police, and that leads, slowly but shockingly, to them turning their suspicion onto Nick himself. In *The Goldfinch* thirteen-year-old Theo Decker and his mother, visiting an art gallery, are caught in an explosion that kills her, and in that horrifying moment that utterly upsets the balance of Theo's life, he grabs a painting, an inchoate impulse springing from his need for a thread of connection to his mother, and an action that will haunt him for years, through all the twists of this big story.

Note: the inciting event must affect the life of the protagonist in a way they are *aware* of. It cannot be an "off-stage" occurrence, however significant (for example, the outbreak of war), if it has no personal impact on the character.

In *Gone With the Wind* the book's opening section does indeed include the outbreak of civil war, which is, of course, a hugely important event in objective terms. But characters, like real people, are not objective. What matters to Scarlett subjectively—and what incites her to action—is not the war itself but that the war pushes Ashley to marry Melanie before he leaves for his regiment. That's what spurs Scarlett to make the rash decision to marry Charles.

Try to have your inciting incident happen as close to your story's opening as possible, but don't rush it. It does not have to be on page one. (Some novels, for example, open with an event involving the story's antagonist.) It should, however, almost certainly occur within the first twenty pages or so. The most important thing is to give your reader someone to care about right away. Then, when the time is ripe, bring on the incident that upsets the balance of the main character's life and rouses them to take an action.

Write a powerful inciting incident, and "it must follow as the night the day" that your characters will lead you headlong onto their conflict, into their world, and into a compelling story.

3. OVERARCHING STORY QUESTION

Every well-constructed story poses, at the outset, an implicit question that carries the action along from the inciting incident to the resolution of the conflict. How, the reader wonders, will this turn out? This is the overarching story question. It's not, of course, an actual sentence ending with a question mark, but rather a conundrum that's raised, engaging the reader's need to know the answer. The question hovers throughout the story, keeping the reader in suspense. An analogy is a juggler tossing balls into the air, manipulating them from one position to another, never letting them fall, constantly building tension in the viewer.

A story's overarching question will always be a straightforward question, not an ambiguous one. Here are three examples:

Presumed Innocent. Scott Turow's complex and powerful mystery novel reverberates with the inner workings of the law and its psychology, and sets the highest of stakes: life and death. Yet the book's overarching story question is very simple: Will Rusty ever discover who killed Caroline?

Gone With the Wind. Will Scarlett ever win Ashley? This seemingly simple question propels Scarlett O'Hara through all of the saga's wide-ranging events: her cunning and courage at surviving the brutality of the Civil War only to face the ruin of her beloved home, Tara; her heroic measures to save her family and Tara's dependants from starvation, and then to rebuild the plantation; her fierce determination, in the chaos of reconstruction, to make her new lumber enterprise a success. All this, while the question that constantly drives Scarlett on is simply, Will she ever win Ashley?

Shogun. James Clavell's grand adventure is set in Japan in the year 1600, and its overarching story question is: Will John Blackthorne, shipwrecked on page one, ever get his ship back from Lord Toranaga so he can sail home to England? This question carries Blackthorne—and the reader—through the dangerous shoals of political intrigue at Toronaga's court with its rival factions; the storms of the Catholic church's hegemony; the siren-song maneuvering of courtesans of the "pillow world" and their behind-the-scenes power; and the calms of Blackthorne's moving love affair with the noblewoman Mariko. But what always drives him on is simply: Will I get my ship back so I can sail home?

> The overarching question of your story is not answered until the story's resolution. As soon as the question is answered, the story ends.

In *Gone With the Wind* it's a quietly stunning moment for Scarlett when the answer comes. Throughout the whole epic sweep of the book she has believed that Ashley loves her, despite his long marriage to Melanie, and that they will one day be together. That conviction has sustained her. At the book's end, she and Ashley sit at the bedside of the dying Melanie, and it comes upon Scarlett with the force of a revelation that Ashley has always loved Melanie, has never loved Scarlett. Even more of a revelation, Scarlett sees that she has never really loved *him*, that she has deluded herself from the beginning, and that the man she does love is Rhett. She runs home to Rhett, but he walks out on her, a shocking moment for Scarlett, and in the third and most forceful revelation of this powerful climax she realizes that Rhett's rejection does not destroy her, that Tara, the land which is the enduring legacy from her father, has always been her deepest love, and that it is Tara she must turn to now. The overarching question has been answered, so the story ends.

As you write the first, tentative drafts of your storyline, you may not yet have a clear sense of what its overarching question is. But once you have completed a full start-to-finish storyline, you will know the question. As soon as you do, and can put it into one succinct sentence like the examples above, write it out and pin it up by your desk. Look at it every day to keep you on track. It will guide you in making strong strategic choices about character and plot, so you can keep those juggling balls in the air until the story's climax and resolution bring them to rest.

4. REVERSALS

A story is made up of events, and each event must bring change, small or large, into the life of your characters. Here's how it works. Your protagonist, in pursuing his or her goal, takes some action and the result brings a change. A scene brings a small to moderate change. A chapter usually ends with a significant to major change. All these changes occur in the form of reversals.

> Reversal means a change that is *unexpected*. A character takes an action expecting a result, but gets a different result than they anticipated.

The result may or may not surprise the reader; if it does, that's fine, but it's not necessary. What's important—what *is* necessary—is that the result is unexpected by the *character*. This reversal of their expectations forces them to try a new course of action to get what they're after.

Scenes always turn on a reversal. Big scenes turn on big reversals. The biggest scene, the story climax, has the biggest reversal of all.

In Shakespeare's *King Lear,* a reversal bursts out of the very first scene; it's this play's inciting incident, as discussed above. When Lear takes his action—his declaration that he's stepping down and will settle equal thirds of his kingdom on his three daughters once they say how much they love him—he's expecting effusive statements of affection from all three. And, indeed, his two elder daughters eagerly gush. But when it's the turn of his youngest, Cordelia, to speak, Lear gets a startling reversal of his expectations. She refuses, saying "I cannot heave my heart into my mouth." The fury this ignites in Lear hurls him onto a shocking new path of action: he disowns Cordelia on the spot and banishes her.

At the beginning of *Romeo and Juliet,* Romeo is in love with Rosaline—this is Scene 2—and in Scene 5 he crashes the Capulets' party just to see Rosaline. It's a bold and risky act because the Capulets are his family's lethal enemies. Then, at the party he sees Juliet for the first time and falls instantly, thunder-struck, in love with her—"Oh, she doth teach the torches to burn bright!"—forgetting all about Rosaline. The result of Romeo's action is nothing like what he expected, and it launches him onto a whole new path of action: to be with Juliet. The scene has turned.

A reversal doesn't have to be radical to be compelling. In E.M. Forster's novel *A Passage To India,* there's a poignant scene that is not "big," but the revelation it depicts is key to the story's theme, and is very moving. The story is set in India in the 1920s against the backdrop of the British Raj and the Indian independence movement. Doctor Aziz is a young Indian Muslim physician, and as this scene opens, one thing the reader already knows about him is that he doesn't much care for the British. As he has told his lawyer friend, some of the Brits are quite "good fellows" when they first come out from London, but they soon become clannish, retreat into their clubs, and snub the Indians. He says he gives an Englishman two years before this happens. The women he gives two months.

Then, one night, Dr. Aziz is all alone in the courtyard of a mosque. He's standing in the moonlight, looking out at the river, feeling the tranquility and peace of the place. Then he hears a rustling behind him, like dead leaves. He turns, and thinks he sees a ghost. The figure steps out of the shadows: an elderly Englishwoman, Mrs. Moore. The reader already knows Mrs. Moore but Aziz does not. Each is startled by the other. Aziz angrily tells her to get out, to not profane this sacred place, saying she has not taken off her shoes.

She points out that she *has* taken off her shoes, and humbly asks if she may therefore be allowed to stay. He grudgingly relents, saying that, yes, of course, she is allowed, it's just that so few English ladies take the trouble because they think, "No one is here, no one will know." She replies, "God is here." That strikes Aziz deeply. He repeats her words in admiration, "God is here." He asks her name, and they begin to talk. And they have an immediate rapport, this old, English, Christian lady and young, Indian, Muslim man. They discover they are both widowed, and that each has two sons and a daughter. Aziz experiences a small revelation: a true reversal of his expectations. It charms the reader, and it's key to the issues of the novel.

Another fine example of a reversal—two, in fact, in the same scene—occurs in *Gone With the Wind*. Scarlett is desperate for money. She'll lose her property, Tara—everything she owns— unless she can scrape together enough cash to pay the taxes. So she visits Rhett Butler in jail, knowing he has made lots of money as a successful privateer. Rhett is enjoying a pleasant incarceration: he plays poker and drinks brandy with the Yankee captain who's his jailer. When Scarlett arrives to see Rhett, she acts carefree, at her most charming, as if life couldn't be better, and tells him she felt such pity at hearing he was in jail, she felt the least she could do was visit him. He buys it, and in fact is delighted to see her. She chats gaily, building her rapport with him. Then Rhett notices her hands. They're calloused and blistered from field work of the toughest kind: picking cotton. He challenges her about it: she's been lying. (First reversal of her expectations.) Caught in her lie, Scarlett takes a new tack. She admits that things are terrible, in fact as bad as they could be. She's desperate for cash, she says, and has come to ask him for a loan. Rhett almost laughs. That incenses Scarlett. "It's not funny," she says. Rhett says, "Actually, it is, because you came for nothing, my dear. I'm stone cold broke." Scarlett's hopes are dashed. (Second reversal of her expectations.) She sweeps out, head high, but from this point on she'll have to try a radical new path to achieve her goal.

5. TURNING POINTS

Major reversals are called turning points. They literally *turn* the story, sending it into a whole new direction. Why? Because the protagonist, in trying to achieve their goal, meets such hugely unexpected obstacles, they must literally turn to taking a new approach to get what they want. Let's look at four examples.

In Peter Benchley's novel *Jaws*, made into the blockbuster film directed by Stephen Spielberg, the central character is police chief Brodie and he is faced with a monster shark that keeps killing people. Nothing he has tried has stopped the shark. So Brodie, facing his own terror, decides, finally, that he must go out on the water himself to try to kill the shark. That decision is a turning point. The story turns, moving to a new location—the ocean—plus a more intense level of personal action, and a new dramatic plateau.

In *Gone With the Wind*, the Civil War's horrors have left Scarlett O'Hara and her family facing starvation. At this, the lowest point in Scarlett's life (it's at the half-way point in the book) she is on her knees, using her bare hands to claw a radish from the ground, like a wild animal. She crams it in her mouth, dirt and all, then vomits, bent and broken. Then, slowly, she pulls herself together, and forces herself to her feet. She raises her fist to the heavens and makes a vow: "As God is my witness, I'm going to live through this ... If I have to steal or kill, as God is my witness, I'm never going to be hungry again." And she never is. From this turning point, Scarlett's journey launches onto a remarkable a new path.

A third example occurs in Robert Harris's political thriller *An Officer and a Spy*, set in Paris in 1895 during the true, infamous miscarriage of justice known as the Drefyus affair. Alfred Dreyfus was convicted of spying and sent to the brutal prison of Devil's Island. The novel's central character, Major Georges Picquart, has been a lifelong loyal soldier in the French Army, but he suspects that Dreyfus is innocent. When Picquart decides to privately investigate, his action puts him on a collision course with powerful army generals and the French government. Picquart could simply drop the matter, but he doesn't. His decision to risk his career, and even his life, by continuing his investigation is a major turning point.

A final example is Donna Tartt's Pulitzer Prize-winning novel *The Goldfinch*. Thirteen-year-old Theo Decker, after the death of his mother, is sent to Las Vegas to live with his deadbeat dad, who betrays him, trying to get at Theo's trust fund. When his father dies, Theo knows he must leave town immediately or be sent to a foster home. It's a turning point that sends Theo on a frightening cross-country bus trip back to New York to seek the people who might help him. Again, as in *Jaws*, the story is launched into a new location as well as a newly intensified personal drama.

Constructing Scenes

Everything I've said above about reversals and turning points deals with the workings of a scene, so this is a good time to look more closely at scene construction.

Scenes are the building blocks of a novel. There will be scenes of varying length (short, medium, long) and varying impact, but every compelling novel is built around a handful of "big scenes"—the turning point scenes—and will have four at a minimum: the inciting incident, the climax of Act I, the climax of Act II, and the climax of Act III, which is also the story's climax. Most novels will have a few more big scenes. All these big scenes are interwoven with smaller scenes.

> Scenes render events. In a scene something *happens*.

That may sound simplistic, but it's helpful to keep in mind so you don't fool yourself into believing that a character staring out a window and thinking is a scene. It's not. In a scene something *happens*.

Here's where creating a step-outline, and updating it as you write your novel's drafts, is invaluable, because it forces you to distil the action of each scene into one line. (See the step-outline for my novel *The Queen's Exiles* at the end of Chapter 4.) So, if you write "John ponders what to do" as a scene, it will become obvious that this is not a scene at all, it's only a beat of a scene. To expand it into a scene the sentence would have to become something like: "John ponders what to do, then tells Jane he's leaving her." Or "John ponders what to do, then digs up the stolen gold." Or "John ponders what to do, then calls the police." You get the idea. In fact, a step outline is not the place to note any character's ponderings, which are simply part of their inner life, their inscape.

So, what, exactly, constitutes a scene?

> A scene is an event that brings change, small or large, into the life of the characters. In every scene, a character pursues a desire, an objective, and this desire will be related to his or her overarching objective that forms the spine of the novel.

Just as a novel has an overarching question that spans the story from inciting incident to climax, each scene will have that same basic structure. In fact, a "big scene" is a story in miniature. The characters have goals, there's an inciting incident, escalating conflict, a reversal, and a climax.

A scene begins by posing an implied question. It gets the reader wondering, quite subconsciously, "How is this going to be resolved? How is this going to work out?" The implied question creates suspense.

The question each scene poses doesn't have to be earth-shaking. To an objective observer it might seem relatively small. But remember, characters in a story are not objective; they have agendas. So the question the scene establishes must wholly engage the character for whom something is at stake. Their motivation kick-starts the scene. Here's an example from my novel *The*

Experiment. This scene opens with David Knelman, an Assistant District Attorney in New York, about to go into court.

> David Knelman strode down the busy hall outside the courtroom at One Hundred Center Street, passing a cluster of black women, one of them crying, likely over some guy in the holding cells. He was heading for a portly, balding, pink-faced man sitting on a bench beside the elevator. Sunday best suit, not new. Battered suitcase on his lap. Looked like a hard-up salesman, David thought. He hoped this man knew his stuff. A magician, apparently well-known on the B nightclub circuit for his sleight-of-hand theatrics, he was to be David's make-or-break witness.

The implicit question posed is: Will David's witness make his case or break it? It sets up the reader to wonder: how will this turn out?

As a scene progresses, it should either answer the implicit question or in some way deal with it. Let me give you an example of a book that does *not* do this. It's a thriller by a well-known author. (Note: a star author can get away with flaws like this because they have established a vast readership that guarantees their publisher vast sales. But a writer seeking to break into the business cannot afford a weakness like the following one.) The book starts with a tense, atmospheric scene of a man in prison receiving a letter. He reads it, and the contents are clearly devastating to him, but the reader is not told what the letter says.

This is excellent suspense. As a reader, I'm excited to know: What's in the letter? So I eagerly read on. In the next chapter, the character re-reads the letter, and again he is deeply disturbed by it, and I really want to find out what's so important about it, but still the author doesn't say. I read on, through more chapters with references to this momentous letter, but since its contents are still annoyingly unknown to me, my patience is thinning. This goes on for *many* chapters: the letter and a sense of its dire portent, but no enlightenment. And pretty soon I'm thinking, tell me what's in the damn letter or I'm closing the book for good.

This kind of suspense is a cheat. The author is merely withholding facts in a stagnant ongoing manipulation of the reader's curiosity. Nothing shifts; nothing changes.

> With every implicit question introduced, the scene should either answer it or deal with it in some significant way. Then, spin a new question.

Another technique for posing an implicit question is to begin the scene with a shock, then backtrack. In *The Godfather*, Mario Puzo's novel about the inner world of the New York mafia in the 1950s, made into the now-classic film, Puzo uses this technique with the famous "horse's head" scene. In the book, the scene begins with Tom Hagen, consigliore to the Godfather, Don Corleone, getting a phone call from Hollywood producer Jack Woltz, with Woltz screaming at him, hysterical. The reader wonders: "What terrible thing has happened?" Then Puzo backtracks and takes us to Woltz waking up in bed, smeared with blood, and seeing, at his feet under the bloodied sheets, the head of his beloved prize stallion. Broken by the horror of it, Woltz realizes that the Godfather is responsible, and that he, Woltz, must now submit to Don Corleone's power, so he makes his hysterical phone call to Tom. By starting with the call, Puzo creates suspense, paving the way toward the scene's shocking climax.

When you're planning a scene, these are three vital questions to ask yourself:

1. Who drives the scene? That is, who activates it, makes it happen?
2. What, specifically, does this person want? What's their goal? Desire for this goal is always the key. In other words, what's the character's objective in this scene? I used to make my living as an actor, and when actors discuss a scene they refer to "playing an objective." I recommend that you do the same. Phrase the objective of your driving character, in each scene, as "to do such-and-such" or "to get such-and-such." For example, "To persuade Hank to stay." Or "To coax information from Judith."
3. What force of antagonism blocks the character's desire or objective? Who is preventing them from achieving what they want?

Now, here's where we're going to dig very deep. There's a mechanism you can use to unleash the power in a scene, and it's this: turn the scene on the value that's at stake. As I've mentioned, reversals turn a scene, but reversals cannot be arbitrary; they must be organic to your characters' lives.

Here's how to do it:

1. Identify the value that's at stake in the scene
2. Turn the scene on that value.

By "value" I mean the emotional/psychological stakes for the characters. Great stories have always turned on timeless human values such as:

- Trust
- Hope
- Fear
- Desire
- Loneliness
- Freedom

- Jealousy
- Love
- Survival
- Respect
- Loyalty

These are enduring values of the human condition. That's a noble concept, and inspiring as such, but the point here, for the writer, is very down-to-earth, and it's this. The energy of this technique has its basis in physics: electricity. That is, positive and negative charges. Once you've identified the value that's at stake, decide whether the scene starts on a positive charge or a negative charge. At the beginning of the scene, is the character's situation charged positively or negatively in relation to the value?

Let's say the value at stake is trust. So, does your scene start on a negative charge (mistrust) or a positive charge (trust)? Then, construct the scene so that you turn the value from one state of charge to its opposite: from mistrust to trust, or from trust to mistrust. If the value at stake in the scene is hope, then turn the scene from hope to despair, or, alternatively, from despair to hope. If the value at stake is loyalty and the scene starts with a positive charge, then by its end it must turn to the negative charge: betrayal.

A big scene that does not turn from positive to negative or from negative to positive in relation to its value charge is a failed scene. It's a flat-line scene. Stagnant. You need to rethink it, then rewrite it with this dynamic in mind. Change the value in the scene from positive to negative or vice versa and you'll produce a rich, emotional experience for your reader.

6. THE CLIMAX

Now, let's look at the final core element of story structure: the climax. All the conflict in your book, all the choices the central character has made under pressure, lead inexorably to this moment, the story's crowning, major reversal. The climax is the scene that brings the final and absolute change into the life of your protagonist. That's because the action they take at this moment is the final choice they make. It's irrevocable. No turning back.

That doesn't mean the climax must be full of clamor and violence. It does mean it must be full of meaning. It might, indeed, be fiercely violent, such as a battle sequence, if that's what your story demands. Or it might be a woman finishing an argument with her husband, packing a suitcase, and walking out the door. That's the climax of Ibsen's play, *A Doll's House*, which caused a sensation when it opened in 1879 (when a nice middle-class wife walking out on her husband was considered a degenerate act, possibly a criminal one). In the context of their individual stories, both these climaxes can have overwhelming impact.

> The most effective climax will contain two seemingly contradictory components: it will have an element of surprise, and will also seem inevitable—inevitable, because it springs from the protagonist's deepest character.

The climax is sometimes called the obligatory scene. The phrase comes from French playwrights of a previous era who referred to "la scène à faire" which means "the scene that must be made." This is the scene in which the protagonist and antagonist finally resolve their conflict one way or another. It *must* occur. If it doesn't, the reader will close the book feeling very unsatisfied. So, "obligatory" is a useful word.

As an example, let's look again at Peter Benchley's *Jaws*, whose story structure is so tight it's instructive for writers to study. (Watch the film, directed by Steven Spielberg, and take notes as you identify the inciting incident, the escalating conflict, the reversals, turning points, and climax.) *Jaws* starts with Sheriff Brodie finding a dead girl on the beach, her body half eaten by a shark. The beach is full of holidaying people, and the sheriff cannot let this happen again. But the shark is known to be bold and insatiable. So the overarching story question is set right at the beginning. Who will win, the sheriff or the shark? A compelling opening. The escalating conflict that follows is equally gripping. But no matter how riveting the middle section of the book, if the story ended before this core conflict were resolved, Benchley's readers would have felt horribly let down. They might have thrown his book across the room in disgust. But Benchley delivers. The climax is a tense contest, *mano a mano*, between these two determined characters—sheriff and shark—Brodie summoning every ounce of his courage and waning strength to confront and defeat the monster.

Keep three-act structure in mind, no matter what length your novel is. An act is made up of many chapters and scenes. Each scene contains at least one small to moderate reversal—that is, an event that brings some kind of unexpected change into the life of the characters. Chapters will end in significant change. An act ends in a major change, a turning point. A well-constructed novel will have at least four such turning points: the inciting incident, the climax of Act One, climax of Act Two, and climax of Act Three which is also the story climax. Each turning point must be more forceful than the ones that came before it, all progressively building in intensity to the story climax.

The story climax acts as a catharsis for the reader. The word catharsis stems from the Greek verb meaning "to purify, purge." In his *Poetics*, Aristotle used it to describe the cleansing effect of emotional release that drama has on an audience. If someone reading your book is deeply moved by the story's ending, its climax, you'll leave them feeling as though they have lived through a profound experience. They'll close the book reluctantly, wishing it didn't have to end.

Then, perhaps, they'll hunger to read your next page-turner.

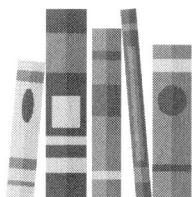

PART III

STYLE

CHAPTER 6

GIVING VOICE: THE ART OF CRAFTING DIALOGUE

"If it sounds like writing, I rewrite it."
ELMORE LEONARD

S ome people can't wait to speak. Some people would almost rather die than speak. Sometimes people don't say what they mean. Sometimes they don't mean what they say. And sometimes their emotions are so raw they can't manage more than a tight word or two. All of this makes dialogue exciting to write and stimulating to read, because characters, like real people, reveal much about themselves by what they say, how they say it, and what they leave unsaid.

In fiction, dialogue is the only instance where there is no barrier between reader and character, no interference from the author giving descriptions and explanations. There is just the character expressing their unique voice, exposing themselves by their words. That's why readers respond intensely to dialogue, and why so many popular novels rely heavily on dialogue.

It feels alive.

UNSPOKEN WORDS

But remember, people don't always say what they mean. Actors have a name for the hidden current running beneath a character's words: subtext. Subtext is what a character *really* means, which can be quite contrary to what they say. Iconic theater director Martha Henry, discussing rehearsals of her production of Arthur Miller's play *All My Sons*, said the actors mined the drama in "scenes where each person on stage is actually talking about something just under the surface of the situation, connected only to his or her character."

Look at the phrase, "I love you." What does a person really mean when they say, "I love you"? The subtext might be any one of the following:

- Forgive me.
- I wish I didn't love you.
- Don't leave me.
- You're lucky to have me.
- Stop nagging me.
- I forgive you.

And you can likely think of a dozen more possible meanings.

In Robert McKee's popular screenwriting seminar he talks about subtext in the classic film *Casablanca* starring Humphrey Bogart as Rick Blaine and Ingrid Bergman as Ilsa Lund. McKee refers to the scene in which Ilsa first comes into Rick's crowded café accompanied by her husband. Rick and Ilsa have a passionate past: they were lovers, but they parted in desperate circumstances and have not seen each other since that fraught separation. Ilsa's husband knows none of this. In the scene, as Rick and Ilsa meet again face-to-face, they are surrounded by customers gaily socializing, including Ilsa's oblivious husband, and McKee says: "For Rick and Ilsa the text is cocktail chatter; the subtext is molten passion." Hidden passion is what those two actors, Bogart and Bergman, are playing.

In writing a novel, of course, there are no actors to convey the characters' feelings. Instead, the writer must do so—must convey the suppressed passion, or simmering anger, hurt pride, delight, jealousy, anxiety, curiosity, disgust, surprise, sorrow, pity, shame, or any other emotion—though the characters may say none of it explicitly.

Inexperienced writers often make the mistake of writing subtext as dialogue. That is, they'll have characters say *exactly* what they're thinking and feeling. This is called writing "on the nose." It's heavy handed, and does nothing to reveal *deep* meaning. For example, imagine if the writers of *Casablanca* put Rick's tortured feelings into dialogue like this: "I can't bear it, Ilsa. I hate you for how you hurt me, but I still love you, and I want you so bad it's killing me." Sounds horribly unrealistic and melodramatic, doesn't it?

Don't force subtext into dialogue. Layer subtext into narration.

Layering the subtext into narration requires finesse. I offer here an excellent example, an excerpt, somewhat abridged, from Ian McEwan's novel *Atonement*. The book's opening section is set in an English country house in 1935, and in this scene the family and their visitors are sitting down to dinner during a stultifying heat wave. Some of them are at ease, some are not. Two of them, Robbie Turner and Cecilia Tallis, are in a turmoil of private excitement, having just had fast and furious sex for the first time in a nook of the library. Cecilia's thirteen-year-old sister Briony had, in horrified confusion, glimpsed them.

> Leon muttered a short suspended grace—For what we are about to receive—to which the scrape of chairs was the amen ... Silence followed ... Emily Tallis had always been incapable of small talk and didn't much care. Leon, entirely at one with himself, lolled in his chair, wine bottle in hand, studying its label. Cecilia was lost to the events of ten minutes before and could not have composed a simple sentence. Robbie was familiar with the household and would have started something off, but he too was in turmoil. It was enough that he could pretend to ignore Cecilia's bare arm at his side—he could feel its heat—and the hostile gaze of Briony who sat diagonally across from him. And even if it had been considered proper for children to introduce a topic, they too would have been incapable: Briony could think only of what she had witnessed.

It was Paul Marshall who broke the more than three minutes of asphyxiating silence. He moved back in his chair to speak behind Cecilia's head to Robbie.

"I say, are we still on for tennis tomorrow?"

Out of politeness Robbie too had moved back in his seat to hear the remark, but even in his state he flinched. It was inappropriate, at the beginning of the meal, for Marshall to turn away from his hostess and begin a private conversation.

Robbie said tersely, "I suppose we are," and then, to make amends for him, added for general consideration, "Has England ever been hotter?"

There are just three brief lines of dialogue, and they're practically meaningless on the face of the words, but the narration is packed with the characters' private, intense emotions. Look how many emotions course through Robbie.

Here's another example. This one is from Giles Blunt's novel *Forty Words for Sorrow*. John Cardinal is a detective in his forties in a small Ontario city. His wife Catherine is in the hospital bring treated for clinical depression, and his teenage daughter, Kelly, is away in New York studying art. Here's a brief phone conversation Cardinal has with his daughter. Note how expertly Blunt slides Cardinal's subtext into the narration.

"Hi, Kelly. How's school going?" So plain, so flat. Why can't I call her Princess or Sweetheart the way fathers do on TV? Why can't I say the place is colder without you? Without Catherine?

Why not tell her this tiny house is suddenly the size of an airport?

"I'm working on a humungous project for my painting class, Daddy. Dale's taught me that I work best on a monumental scale, not on the crabbed little canvases I always stuck with before. It's like being set free. I can't tell you how good it feels. My work is a hundred times better."

"Sounds good, Kelly. Sounds like you're enjoying it." That's what he said. What he thought was: God it moves me to hear you're happy, to hear that you're growing, that your life is full and good.

Kelly chattered on about learning at last how to wield paint, and normally Cardinal would have basked in her enthusiasm. In the course of his sleepless night he had stood in the doorway of her bedroom and stared at the narrow bed she had slept in for a week, picked up the paperback she had been reading, just to touch something his daughter had touched.

It's important that you don't leave your reader in the dark about characters' subtext. Inexperienced writers often make this mistake, leaving it out of the narration completely. I come across this frequently in reviewing emerging writers' manuscripts. I think it's because they're relying on how they hear and see the scene in their head, as though they're watching a lively film. No wonder: ours is a film culture; we're saturated by films. But a novel is not a film. In a film there is an actor skillfully showing every nuance of emotion, giving rich life to dialogue that might reveal nothing on the words' surface. The actor is playing the subtext, and the viewer sees it. A film also gets the potent boost of a music score composed to stir specific emotions in the viewer. But that experience does not exist for the reader of a novel. The novelist does not enjoy the luxury of having an actor effortlessly reveal complex meaning with a single look, and a musical score to emphasize it. When subtext is necessary, the novelist must write it, write the character's precise thoughts and feelings. Imagine the scene above stripped of its written subtext. It would be Cardinal simply saying, "Hi, Kelly. How's school going?" and Kelly chattering on about her art, without the author giving us Cardinal's emotional state as he listens. The reader would have no hint of the love Cardinal longs to convey with his words, but can't.

Writing subtext is actually one of the novelist's joys, because we get to show *exactly* what a character is thinking and feeling. In fact, the novelist should pity the screenwriter, who is restricted to just two tools on the page: dialogue and action. After that, the screenwriter has to pray for good actors to reveal the characters' hidden depths. The novelist has far more leeway. You can show your reader the characters' precise inner lives, what's going through their heads and hearts, no matter how spare their spoken words. That's the rich experience that keeps readers turning pages.

FUNCTIONS OF DIALOGUE

Writing dialogue is fun, because it's so charged with life, which is why so many popular novels rely heavily on it. Fun aside, though, a strictly analytical examination of the functions of dialogue is worthwhile so you can use this tool of craft to best effect. Here are four basic functions that dialogue performs.

Function #1: To move the story forward.

There are countless ways that dialogue does this. A character might reveal information to someone, or admit to knowledge. They might incite another character to act. They might make accusations, lie about something, defend themselves, argue their reasons, distract their listener, deny important facts—the possibilities are endless. The point is this: all stories are about conflict, and good dialogue will always add some degree of tension, be it minimal, moderate, or extreme. In other words, there should be no idle chit-chat—unless, of course, the chit-chat is masking serious subtext that you're conveying in the narration.

Function #2: To establish relationships.

People speak differently to different people. For example, if you were telling your ten-year-old niece about something you learned from this book, you would articulate it, in content and vocabulary, in a way very different than you would if you were telling a fellow writer. Relationships take on unique life through dialogue. They become more real than they could ever be just through narrative. Because dialogue makes characters come alive, the relationships between them spring to life too. Knowing this, you can use passages of dialogue strategically, to highlight characters' relationships.

Function #3: To give the impression of natural speech.

Here's the challenge: dialogue should look and sound like natural speech, but not be an actual reproduction of natural speech, because natural speech is muddled. It isn't fluid. It starts and stops. It wanders. People halt phrases half-way through to re-think them, and then come up with a new phrase. If you sit down in a coffee shop and listen to the people behind you talking (and I hope you do this often; we writers are magpies, gathering bits of chaff with which to build) you'll hear conversations that are completely disjointed. Things like:

> "Really? You sure they all—"
> "Not then, but—"
> "Well, how would he ... like, if he has—"
> "That's just it. I've always said—"
> "But he wasn't at—"
> "No, I mean the *dinner*."
> "Oh, yeah, right. No, I don't know ... it's too—"
> "Exactly!"

For those two people, who know all the private context and are looking each other in the eye, it makes perfect sense, but if you wrote a long sequence of garbled dialogue like that it would be virtually unreadable. Instead, as writers we strive to give the *feel* of natural speech, not to reproduce it exactly.

Function #4: To illuminate a character's individuality.

The goal is to create dialogue that is character-specific. That is, each character speaks in their unique fashion. To achieve this, it's helpful to think as an actor thinks; to develop an actor's ear for people's speech patterns. The vocabulary a person uses, the syntax of their speech, their grammar—all of it reveals a great deal about them. For example, the pedantic speech of an English professor is vastly unlike the jargon of a kid living on the street. Look at the different ways people express simple agreement. Someone might say, "Yes." For another it's "Sure thing." Or "Cool." Or "Whatever." Or "You got that right." Or "Splendid notion." Or "Fuckin' A!" Each of these is just a declaration of agreement (and I'm sure you can think of many more) but each reveals something unique about who is saying it.

It's also effective to pepper a character's speech judiciously with idioms to individualize them—words or phrases that are peculiar to that person alone. For example, the military man who, for praise, always uses the one-word statement "Outstanding." In the film *The Princess Bride,* much loved for its comedy, the Wallace Shawn character, who has a bit of a lisp, is always saying, "It's incon*ceiv*able!" In John Irving's novel *The Cider House Rules,* Dr. Larch repeatedly refers to his collection of orphan boys as "You princes of Maine, you kings of New England." He loves saying the phrase, and the reader loves hearing it. It's part of the doctor's charm.

Body Language

Gestures and body language are a living part of dialogue. For example, instead of answering a barbed question, a person might look away. By punctuating a sequence of dialogue with a character's body language you can reveal some facet of their feelings. A woman fidgets with her wedding ring. A man rakes his hand through his hair. A girl covers her mouth to hide a smile. Such gestures also give rhythm to a scene, filling the silences between the characters' spoken lines. This fine-tunes the scene's pacing.

Here's a good example from Joanna Trollope's novel *The Best of Friends.* At this point in the story, Fergus, a decorator of astute artistic taste, has moved out of the family home, leaving his wife and teenage daughter Sophy, and this scene opens with Sophy visiting him in his new home. Note the gestures and body language.

"I'm here," Sophy said.

Fergus stared at her.

"Sophy—"

He held the door with one hand and in the other he held his reading glasses, half-moon spectacles framed in tortoiseshell. His hair stood on end a bit, as if he'd ruffled it while he was thinking.

"My dear, how wonderful. How—it's just that I wasn't expecting you."

Sophy hitched her bag a little higher on her shoulder.

"May I come in?"

"Of course," he said. "Of course—" He sounded flustered. He stood back, holding the door open for her, and as she went past he made a small clumsy dart to kiss her cheek, and missed.

She went into the sitting room and dumped her bag on a white sofa. He followed her.

"Did you get my letter?"

"Of course," she said, her eyes widening. "Why else do you think I'm here?"

"It's—it's just that I didn't think it would be quite so soon."

"I had to," Sophy said simply.

Fergus went across to the white sofa and transferred her bag to the floor.

"New covers—"

Sophy made a little impatient noise. She bent over a table with some glass and silver objects on it and re-arranged them, asserting her right to do that in retaliation for having her bag shifted. Fergus moved quickly beside her and put his hand restrainingly on hers.

"Sophy, why did you have to?"

She looked at him. "You said we had to look at flats. And schools. School starts again next week."

Fergus sighed. "Dear one, we can't get you into a new school this term. It would have to be after Christmas—"

"Why would it?"

"It's too late now—"

"But I don't want to do just two terms somewhere. I want to do a proper year—"

"Sophy," Fergus said, seizing both her wrists, "Stop this nonsense. Stop being so damned childish. Tell me why you have suddenly turned up here, out of the blue."

She glared.

"You asked me to come."

"I know. But you know as well as I do that I didn't mean by return of post."

Common Errors

Here are three faults to avoid when writing dialogue.

#1. Using dialogue to deliver exposition.

Exposition is factual information the writer needs the reader to know. The *least* effective way to render it is through dialogue. It's the cardinal sin in writing dialogue. To make the point, here's a ridiculous example. A scientist is telling a colleague about the project they've been working on together, and says, "As you're aware, John, it's imperative that we find the XR5 submarine before those nuclear warheads—the ones we know are aimed at San Francisco—get into the hands of the Green Crescent. You know, that suicide bomber cell that killed your wife and kids last Christmas." Avoid this.

Bad films are notorious for forcing exposition into dialogue. Like this. The phone rings. The character picks it up and hears: "Hi, Steve, it's your co-worker, Gerry." I can feel you wince, so you get it. People do not talk this way; they do not say things they know the other person knows. Screenwriters, of course, face a huge challenge in delivering exposition, because the only tools they have on the page are dialogue and action; there is no narration. But novelists have no excuse for forcing exposition into dialogue. We can just slide it into the narration, like this: "Steve answered the phone. It was Gerry from work. 'Hi, man.'" There, we get the information about the relationship, and the colleague's name, but it's not forced into dialogue.

In his book *Story,* written for screenwriters, Robert McKee offers this helpful rubric: "Convert exposition to ammunition." He goes on: "Your characters know their world, their history, each other, and themselves. Let them use what they know as ammunition in their struggle to get what they want."

For example, instead of making a character—let's call her Louise—deliver exposition such as "Angie, how long have we been best friends? About fifteen years, right? Ever since those days together in drama school," the screenwriter might convert that exposition into ammunition, like this, following Louise's glance at Angie's haggard face and too-bleached hair: "Angie, you're a mess. Still hoping for the big break, still dating loser directors, still trotting out the same audition piece from our last show in drama school." The viewer will be caught up in watching Angie's pained reaction, but will hear "drama school" and sense that those school days were some years ago.

Luckily, the novelist faces no such constraints, because a novel has narration in which to deliver exposition. Nevertheless, the wise novelist will employ McKee's screenwriting rubric, since every choice you make about what your characters say and do should be at the service of them living their lives, trying to achieve what they want, dealing with whatever force of antagonism obstructs them. Cramming exposition into their spoken words does nothing to illuminate their struggle.

Dialogue is as fragile as breath. It cannot be expected to carry the heavy weight of exposition. Lay exposition on the broad shoulders of narration.

Fault #2. Using extravagant verbs for dialogue attribution.

Dialogue attribution is the "he said" or "she said" part of a dialogue sequence, indicating which character is speaking. It's often referred to as a "dialogue tag." An inexperienced writer will often use an exaggerated verb, believing it helps the reader hear the character's tone of voice. "Go to hell," he *raged*. "Stop," she *hissed*. "No," he *snarled*, or *thundered*, or *howled*. " (Mary Shura Craig advises: "Unless a character has more than two legs, he isn't convincing when barking, snarling, or growling.") Stephen King calls this practice "shooting the attribution verb full of steroids."

More importantly, overwrought verbs like these call attention to themselves instead of to the character. And that slip-up is what John Gardiner rightly calls one of the chief mistakes a writer can make: "To allow or force the reader's mind to be distracted, even momentarily, from the fictional dream."

Have trust that readers will know how your characters are speaking because they have a sense of the characters' personalities and the situation. My advice for dialogue attribution is this: stick mostly to "said" and "asked" and a few nuanced variations like "explained" and "replied." If you simply can't resist the lure of a pumped-up verb for attribution (and I confess to sometimes succumbing to their seduction), I recommend that you limit yourself to one or two per chapter.

Sometimes the reason emerging writers get overly creative with verbs for dialogue attribution is because they think the word "said" lacks punch and personality. Also, they fear that repeating "said" over and over will annoy the reader. In fact, the opposite is true. The word "said" is a miracle word. The miracle is that the reader's eye skips right over it; it's almost invisible. The brain takes in the name of the speaker and unconsciously ignores the verb "said." The same is true for neutral verbs like "asked" and "replied." Here's the advice of author Elmore Leonard, a master of dialogue: "Never use a verb other than 'said' to carry dialogue.

The line of dialogue belongs to the character; the verb is the author sticking his nose in ... I once noticed Mary McCarthy ending a line of dialogue with 'she asseverated' and had to stop reading to get the dictionary."

Of course, there are exceptions to every rule. A delicious one is Hollywood producer Linda Obst's cheeky non-fiction book about Hollywood titled *Hello, He Lied.*

Fault #3. Writing heavy dialect.

Dialect means rendering a character's speech in an irregular way, not like normal speech. A writer might want to point up the irregularity of speech from, say, a waitress with a deep southern drawl, or a Russian immigrant, or a homeboy from the 'hood. The fault here is to write dialect by using a lot of phonetic spelling—that is, spelling by the sound rather than using normal spelling. A one-word example is "whacha" instead of "what do you." It draws undue attention to itself, and that yanks the reader out of the experience, the fictional dream. Also, sequences of dialect are difficult to read, making the reader struggle to decipher the phonetic spellings. If dialect goes on and on, it can exhaust the reader.

Instead, give just the *flavor* of dialect. Merely suggest it with a few strategic words or phrases, and then continue with normal spelling. Have faith that readers will know how the character pronounces something because they know the character and context. For example, a simple "Yo!" or "I reckon" will suggest volumes about a character. After that introduction to them, there's no need to write out phonetically everything they say. Readers are smart; they'll get it. Or, let's say you're writing a character who is Russian and speaks English poorly. The Russian language doesn't use articles ("the" and "a") as English does, so all you have to do is write this character's dialogue without articles: "I put book on table." That simple linguistic tip-of-the-hat to readers will let them carry on and do the rest of the mental work themselves, and with far less effort than struggling over phonetically rendered dialect.

A good way to test the dialogue you've written is to read it aloud. Potholes and speed bumps that you might gloss over when silently reading your characters' words will become apparent when you speak them. An author friend of mine actually hires an actor to read aloud to him the dialogue passages in his manuscripts. That's a terrific idea, if you can afford it. But even reading your dialogue aloud by yourself will yield discoveries of what to cut and what to polish.

INDIRECT DIALOGUE

All the discussion above about dialogue refers to *direct* dialogue: a character's spoken words placed inside quotation marks. But writers can also make effective use of *indirect* dialogue. Indirect dialogue is a summary of what a character says, and does not appear between quotation marks. You might choose to put some information into indirect dialogue, because direct dialogue isn't always necessary even if the information contained in it is. Note this little gem of economy from Rex Burns's mystery *The Killing Zone* in which he skates over facts exchanged between the characters, facts that are important for them to cover but would be tedious to read if they spoke it all.

> "What was his schedule for Wednesday?"
> She told him, pointing to the calendar and explaining its abbreviations. In addition to

routine committee work, meetings, and functions, he had a dozen-or-so visitors to talk to.
"Is that usual?"

So, indirect dialogue can be an economical way to move
the scene forward quickly while still letting the reader know
that a more lengthy discussion is happening. You might also
use indirect dialogue to change a scene's pacing, or to break up
a long sequence of direct dialogue. Making this choice, as so
often happens with our craft, is the difference between showing
and telling. Direct dialogue *renders* speech (showing it) while
indirect dialogue simply *relates* speech (telling it). Although
showing is usually preferable, there are times when telling is
more effective. The following are two examples. The first is from
the climax scene of Jane Austen's *Pride and Prejudice*, published
in 1813. Elizabeth and Darcy, after their book-long frustrations
with each other—misunderstandings, outright insults, and blun-
ders—finally declare their love. It happens in small bursts of
discovery. Darcy is the first to affirm how he feels, and he does
so in urgent, direct dialogue. But Elizabeth is too startled, and
pleased, to say a word in response. Darcy goes on:

> "You are too generous to trifle with me. If your
> feelings are still what they were last April, tell
> me so at once. My affections and wishes are
> unchanged, but one word from you will silence
> me forever."
> Elizabeth, feeling all the more than com-
> mon awkwardness and anxiety of his situation,
> now forced herself to speak; and immediately,

though not very fluently, gave him to understand that her sentiments had undergone so material a change since the period to which he alluded, as to make her receive with gratitude and pleasure his present assurances. The happiness which this reply produced was such as he had probably never felt before, and he expressed himself as sensibly and warmly as a man violently in love can be supposed to do.

Note how Elizabeth's response is given in indirect dialogue (she "gave him to understand") and so is Darcy's immediate reaction (he "expressed himself"). This technique allows Austen to distill the intense moment between the lovers into a few words and thus maintain the quick pace of their shared discovery, a pace that matches their quickened emotions. When they do speak aloud again, their words have sudden vigor, giving the scene dramatic energy.

The second example of indirect dialogue is from John Steinbeck's masterpiece *East of Eden*.

Samuel began to talk to push the silence away. He told how he had first come to the valley fresh from Ireland, but within a few words neither Cathy nor Adam was listening to him. To prove it, he used a trick he had devised to discover whether his children were listening when they begged him to read to them and would not let him stop. He threw in two sentences of nonsense. There was no response from either Adam or Cathy. He gave up.

Talk Plus Action

One last point about writing dialogue. It's wise to avoid long scenes of merely "talking heads"—that is, continuous talk from the characters with nothing else going on. A solution is to introduce a background action that one or more of the characters is busy with. Bestselling mystery author Elizabeth George has a clever term for this, which she suggests in her book *Write Away*. She calls the technique a "Talking Head Avoidance Device"— T.H.A.D. for short. For example, as two characters carry on a long sequence of talk, a T.H.A.D might be that one is washing the dog. Or weeding the garden. Picking up a child's toys. Grooming a horse. Assembling a rifle. The choices are endless.

But choose strategically. The action you pick can supply much more than just relief in pacing. It gives you another opportunity to reveal character. So choose your T.H.A.D. to be symbolic. Here's an example from my novel *The Queen's Lady*, set in 16th-century England during the reign of Henry VIII. Henry's chancellor was Sir Thomas More, and I invented a fictional character, Honor Larke, to be his ward. I set a crucial, turning point scene between these two inside More's menagerie of exotic animals (he really did have such a menagerie) and in the dialogue Honor anxiously presses him for information about her friend who's been executed. As a T.H.A.D., I had More blithely strolling past the caged creatures and stopping to coax food at a blank-eyed, emaciated monkey. I chose this activity so that the captive animals' whimpers serve as a thematic counterpoint to the dialogue, underscoring Honor's dawning horror that More himself was behind her friend's death.

Another example is a film I recall (though not its title) in which a quiet guy who's a tattoo artist has recently met a girl and they're attracted to each other but both are shy, so the writer set their "first date" scene at a party where the guy has his gear and offers to give the girl a shoulder tattoo. As he starts, they make awkward small talk. That's the dialogue. But the tattoo procedure requires constant touching, constant eye contact to check levels of pain or pleasure, so the small talk is erotically charged. It's a perfect strategic choice of T.H.A.D. on the part of the writer.

Enjoy all the delights and rewards of writing dialogue. And, always, listen carefully to people. Develop an actor's ear. Hear what's left unsaid. As Henry James wrote, "Try to be one of those on whom nothing is lost."

CHAPTER 7

CREATING WORLDS
WITH WORDS

*"For your born writer, nothing is so healing as the
realization that he has come upon the right word."*

CATHERINE DRINKER BOWEN

In writing a book, you create a whole world. You build it
with words.

The English language is rich in the sheer number of words,
250,000 at least, according to the Oxford Dictionary. Shakespeare
is responsible for quite a few; he invented hundreds of words.
He did it by changing nouns into verbs, changing verbs into
adjectives, using old words in new ways, and devising wholly
original words. An example of a noun made into a verb is in his
play *Measure for Measure*. When Vincentio, the Duke of Vienna,
takes a leave of absence and appoints Angelo as his deputy,
someone later comments that, "Lord Angelo dukes it well."

Many of our everyday expressions originated in Shakespeare's plays. Brave new world. Foul play. Foregone conclusion. Into thin air. Rhyme and reason. Too much of a good thing. You're quoting Shakespeare if you've ever said that someone played fast and loose, if you've been tongue-tied, or a tower of strength, or hoodwinked, or in a pickle; if you have knitted your brows, made a virtue of necessity, slept not one wink, stood on ceremony; if you have seen better days, or lived in a fool's paradise. It's all Shakespeare.

We're still inventing words, and new ways of using words. How do you find out about someone online? You Google them. Social media tech words abound: crowdsourcing, hashtag, spam, troll. And in popular culture: BFF, metrosexual, staycation, mockumentary. Language usage is constantly evolving. For example, "they" used as a singular pronoun has long been considered incorrect by grammarians. (Instead of "Everyone wants their child to succeed," purists prefer "Everyone wants his or her child to succeed.") But "his or her" feels cumbersome to most people, and "they" has the added modern appeal of being gender-neutral. It is now ubiquitous. In fact, "they" as a singular pronoun was named Word of the Year at an American linguists' convention in 2016. (I happily use it throughout this book.)

The Washington Post runs an annual competition for its readers to submit alternative meanings to existing words, and the submissions are often delightful. A few of my favorites:

Coffee (n.), the person upon whom one coughs

Flabbergasted (adj.), appalled over how much weight you have gained

Esplanade (v.), to attempt an explanation while drunk

Willy-nilly (adj.), impotent

Negligent (adj.), describes a condition in which you absentmindedly answer the door in your nightgown.

Lymph (v.), to walk with a lisp

Balderdash (n.), a rapidly receding hairline

We often take nouns that are important to us, like body parts, and empower them by making them verbs. She's *headed* in the right direction. They were *necking* in the back seat. Just *mouth* the words. He *shouldered* his way through the crowd. She *elbowed* the guy. Then *kneed* him. The cop *fingered* the thief. She couldn't *stomach* the truth. At the last minute, they *backed* out. You'd better *toe* the line, boy.

We also love making animal names into verbs. The detective *dogged* her suspect. His sister *larked* her way through college. Stop *horsing* around. The creek *snaked* around the gravel pit. The old actor *swanned* into the room. Hey, that kid's *aping* me!

Sensory Images

Writers create imaginary worlds, and to do that most effectively we use concrete images. Like those animal verbs above. The opposite is an abstract image. Brown, for example, is abstract: "brown eyes." But "eyes like wet stones" is concrete. The more concrete the word, the more vivid the image. By using concrete, sensory details we make the reader feel they're right there in the scene. It's almost a trick, and it's always effective. Like the guy who tells a yarn about his improbable adventure and says, "Don't believe me?" adding, as he plucks his shirt collar, "I was wearing this shirt when it happened!" We see the shirt, so we believe. Seeing is believing.

> Word choice is about making your readers see and believe.

But don't stick just to visuals; some of the most vibrant images are sounds, smells, textures, tastes. In *The Sound and the Fury,* William Faulkner wrote, "Caddy smelled like trees." In *The Great Gatsby,* F. Scott Fitzgerald says Daisy's voice is "full of money." Vivid smells pull your reader deep into a scene. For example, let's say you're describing a man in clothes that are damp from rain. If the reader is given just the appearance of those clothes, the man could be across the room, but if they read that the man's sweater gives off the musty, wet-dog smell of damp wool, they're right next to him.

Description, though, is more than facts. The "more" is emotion. As writers we strive to always evoke emotion in the reader, because emotion is the way people understand and remember things. It's how our brains work. We don't remember abstractions, we remember a thing because we feel it. We human beings are not thinking creatures who can feel; we're feeling creatures who can think.

So, to move our readers—to nudge them to feel a character's awe, joy, anger, affection, horror, pity—what words are best? Henry David Thoreau wrote: "As to adjective: when in doubt, strike it out." Don't become a tyrant and banish all adjectives; they're often valuable, even necessary. But do listen to the small inner voice that tells you when they're not: Thoreau's "when in doubt."

Adverbs, too. Stephen King offers this sage, if cheeky, warning: "The road to hell is paved with adverbs." Trust that a scene's context will supply the emotional quality of a character's words and actions far better than an adverb will. For example, you can easily imagine the context that leads to *"Yikes, that's a long way up," he said doubtfully.* So, cut the adverb "doubtfully" and the sentence is stronger; it stands on its own two feet. The same goes for *She twisted the napkin in her fingers anxiously.* The reader, having the scene's full context, will sense the character's emotional state, so that clunky adverb "anxiously" can be cut.

Let nouns and verbs guide your writing. Nouns and verbs together add up to people and things in motion, and a person in motion always raises interest. Also, nouns and verbs often *contain* description. In the sentence *He ambled down the boulevard,* you know the character is relaxed, because no one who is tense can *amble.* And we know he's in a fashionable urban setting, because there are no *boulevards* in the countryside or a slum. Yet the sentence contains no adjectives and no adverbs.

Look at the verbs John Steinbeck uses in *East of Eden* in depicting early morning in a rural town in the 1920s: "The sparrows shrieked over the horse manure ... Big cats would ripple across the street to disappear in the tall grass." And, in the following sentence, instead of *describing* a sound that a character sitting in the dining room hears, Steinbeck *conjures* it: "The cook was fighting with pots in the kitchen."

PLAIN ENGLISH IS BEST

A common fault new writers make is using Latinate words—words that have their origin in Latin. For centuries in England, Latin was the language of the educated classes (the clergy and lawyers), so people who wanted to sound educated used Latinate words, and the habit persists to this day, usually for the same reason: the desire to sound cultured. But Latinate words seldom have the power and clarity of ordinary, everyday English words, Anglo-Saxon words.

Latinate: He *descended* the stairs and *exited* his *abode* where he *encountered* the *female* who *resided* in the neighboring *domicile. Observing* her *magnificent physique* as she passed him, he *contemplated* his *aspiration* to *engage* her in *conversation*, and in *supplementary* acts.

Anglo-Saxon: He *went down*stairs and *left* his *house* where he *came upon* the *woman* who *lived next door. Gazing* at her *buxom form* as she passed him, he thought about how much he wanted to talk to her, and more.

George Orwell, author of *Nineteen-Eighty-Four* and *Animal Farm*, and a master of robust, plain English, said: "A mass of Latin words falls upon the facts like soft snow, blurring the outline and covering up all the details. The great enemy of clear language is insincerity."

The Four "B"s

Here are four recommendations to keep your writing fresh:

Be Concrete.

As noted above, avoid the abstract. If you write, "The dog was enormous," the abstract adjective "enormous" is relative, and therefore almost meaningless. But "The dog was the size of a Shetland pony" is concrete; it's tangible.

Be Specific.

Avoid generalization; choose specific nouns over general ones. It's not merely a bird on a tree limb, it's a blue jay. It's not a car but a "coffee-colored Cadillac," like in the Chuck Berry song.

Here's a paragraph from Tim O'Brien's book *The Things They Carried* about American soldiers in Viet Nam. Notice how much O'Brien achieves through a simple list of concrete, specific things, and how few adjectives (and no adverbs) he uses to describe his characters.

> Until he was shot, Ted Lavender carried six or seven ounces of premium dope, which for him was a necessity. Mitchell Sanders, the RTO, carried condoms. Norman Bowker carried a diary. Pat Kiley carried comic books. Kiowa, a devout Baptist, carried an illustrated New Testament that had been presented to him by his father who taught Sunday school in Oklahoma City, Oklahoma … When Ted Lavender was shot, they used his poncho to wrap him up, then to carry

him across the paddy, then to lift him into the chopper that took him away.

That paragraph has just three descriptive adjectives: "premium", "illustrated" and "devout." Instead, it's full of tangible things, alive with details so striking they enlighten the reader about the character or the setting.

Be Creative.

Avoid clichés. Once, these were concrete words and phrases that evoked a specific image, but they've become so overused they're now abstractions. Chiseled jaw. Any port in a storm. Every cloud has a silver lining. Often clichés are similes: Drinks like a fish. Avoid it like the plague. Light as a feather. Old as the hills. I like the advice of editor Sol Stein: "Say it new, or say it straight."

However, I have one good word to offer about clichés. They can have a useful role as place markers when you're writing a first draft. They let you get through the draft quickly without agonizing over every word and sweating to make every image exact. My advice is don't be overly afraid of clichés; just flag them (in my own writing I often mark them in bold), then move on, and in your final draft, change each one to a fresh image.

Be Careful.

Avoid inaccurate and imprecise words and phrases. "She tossed her head at me." We know what the writer intends to say, but he hasn't said it; he's said something else. Carelessness like this breaks the fragile contract between writer and reader. Like a sleeper startled awake, the reader is jerked out of the story, reminded that it is in fact just a story. You don't want to lose the reader for even a moment. So, be accurate.

SHOW VS. TELL

One bedrock principle of good storytelling is "Show, don't tell." That is, the most vivid way to write something is to show it, not tell it. Things exist in a narrative only to the extent that they *happen.*

Look at the difference between these two descriptions of a man's feelings about his little girl.

> #1 "He loved his daughter dearly."

This is telling. You understand the information, but you don't see it happen so you don't feel it.

> #2 "He took a paper out of his pocket. A cray-
> oned drawing of the dog, Dingo, all brown and
> red loops. He brushed his finger over the tiny
> hole where the paper had been folded so many
> times, it had worn through. He'd looked at that
> drawing every night for three years."

This is showing. You know the man loves his little girl because you see a manifestation of it happen, so you feel it.

Showing is often best done by depicting a person in an action, however brief the action is. Compare these two descriptions:

> #1 "She was generous and kind."

You get the information, but you don't feel it.

> #2 "She stopped at Tim Horton's for her usual: two coffees, double-double, and two chocolate donuts. As she passed the homeless guy beside the parking lot she handed him his morning coffee and donut, then carried on to work."

You get the information (that she's generous and kind) *and* you feel it, because you see the character in action.

Here's a tip, a very effective technique. It's about using the phrase "as if." Compare these two descriptions.

> #1 "She had an unconscious sexuality that was unsettling."

We get it, but it's abstract.

> #2 (from Giles Blunt's novel *Forty Words for Sorrow*) "Delorme had a disturbing tendency to hold your gaze just a little too long. It was as if she'd slipped her hand inside your shirt."

Gives you a sweet shiver, doesn't it?

The "it was as if" technique works like the ploy of a court-room lawyer asking the witness, "Was that before or after you beat your wife?" The furious witness may deny *ever* beating his wife, but once the lawyer has conjured that image it's etched in the listener's mind. As writers, we can do the same thing with "it was as if".

So, showing is always more effective than telling. However, all writing is elliptical. That is, we have to leave some things out; every single detail cannot be shown. If you set out to describe just the room you write in, giving every possible detail, it could take dozens of pages. So the writer must constantly choose what to omit. I call this *literary triage*. Sometimes, it's best to simply sum up in narration.

For example, you might write many pages of a tight, two-character scene that's tense with dialogue and builds to a climax, showing everything that happens between those characters during five minutes. Then you might follow it with one brief paragraph that sums up what happens to them over the next five years. It's because those five minutes changed their lives more profoundly than the five following years.

This is another instance of having to make strategic choices. You choose what's essential to show, and what can just be told. Showing should give your writing vitality, make it feel alive. If, instead, it slows the flow, deadens the pace, then telling is better, so use a passage of "tell" narration to sum up what happens, and then move on.

Setting: Your Story's World

The setting, or settings, of your book—where the story takes place—can be a powerful tool to draw your reader in. In many memorable books setting is intrinsic to the tale, inseparable from it. Here are a few:

- Harper Lee's much-loved *To Kill a Mockingbird*, set in Maycomb County, Alabama, in the 1930s, a place of hardscrabble dust and gin-soaked gentility

- Tony Hillerman's bestselling mysteries set in the American Southwest featuring Lieutenant Joe Leaphorn, a Navajo tribal police officer
- Frank Herbert's sci-fi hit *Dune* with its barren, water-parched planet, Arrakis
- J.K. Rowling's *Harry Potter* books imbued with the mystery and magic of Hogwarts with its sumptuous Great Hall, vast grounds, and Forbidden Forest.

Just as setting is crucial to the overall "world-building" of your book, so too is establishing the settings where individual scenes take place. In coaching writers, I often read manuscripts with scenes that lack a sense of place. The settings may be Day-Glo clear in the movie that's playing in the writer's mind, but a book is not a movie. If you, the writer, do not render the setting, the reader is left adrift, with no bearings. There's an old saying: "If it ain't on the page, it ain't on the stage." Whether a scene takes place in a biker's pool hall or an art gallery atrium, you must give your reader specific details to make them feel they're *in* that place. Make them hear the fluorescent light's buzz above the pool table. Have them smell the art patron's gardenia perfume.

The goal is to create settings that are rich and real, and this goes beyond a mere description of *things*. Here's a paragraph from Raymond Chandler's story "Red Wind."

> There was a desert wind blowing that night. It was one of those hot dry Santa Anas that come down through the mountain passes and curl your hair and make your nerves jump and your skin itch. On nights like that every booze party

ends in a fight. Meek little wives feel the edge
of the carving knife and study their husbands'
necks. Anything can happen. You can even get
a full glass of beer at a cocktail lounge.

When I say that paragraph goes beyond describing *things*,
what I mean is that Chandler doesn't paint a picture of a town's
buildings and its nearby mountains. What he gives us is *people*.
Look at how many people are in those seven brief sentences.
Someone's hair is curling. Someone's skin is itching. Guys are
in fights. There are "meek little wives." There are husbands in
danger of having their necks carved. And there's a cocktail lounge
with beer. The setting is not just a town with desert wind, it's a
place teeming with human life.

FUNCTIONS OF SETTING

Setting has two important functions. The first, and most obvious,
is to create atmosphere. Setting establishes what kind of feeling
the reader will take into the experience of reading the book. It
establishes a mood. To do this, you want to avoid merely *reporting*
a setting. Instead, render it in a way that involves all five senses.
Give us sensory details that make the place unique. As author
Julie Smith says, "Don't tell us it was a pretty day. Show us the
sun glinting through a violet canopy of jacarandas."

There is a psychology of place. It's not just the look of a location that matters to readers. What has even more impact is how
it make them *feel*. A place might make you say, "It gives me the
creeps." Another place might feel soothing, like the sun-warmed
wooden dock at a cottage. Another place might be inspiring,
like a cathedral or the Grand Canyon. The *feel* of it is the key,

its psychological effect on the characters and on the reader. Note how Elizabeth George does this in her mystery *For the Sake of Elena,* painting a backdrop of gloom for this story's characters.

> The fog lay heavily on the city the next morning, a grey blanket of mist that rose like a gas from the surrounding fens ... Cars, lorries, buses, and taxis inched their way along the damp pavements ... Bicyclists slowly swayed through the gloom. Pedestrians huddled into heavy coats and dodged the constant spattering of the drops of condensation that fell from rooflines, window ledges, and trees ... The two days of wind and sunshine might never have existed. Fog had returned like a pestilence in the night. This was Cambridge weather with a vengeance.
>
> "Makes me feel like a case for the tubercular ward," Havers said.

The second function of setting is to reveal character. This is so important, but often not well understood by inexperienced writers. The most powerful way to write a setting is to render it in the *attitude* of the point-of-view (POV) character. Description through POV is a form of character development. A grieving widow will see a field of wildflowers utterly differently than will an eager young lover. A farmer suffering drought will see rain differently than will a picnicker.

So for you, the writer, it's never just wildflowers or rain; it's a chance to reveal something about the character. No setting is neutral, because no character is neutral.

Show us setting by infusing the description with the characters' attitude to what they're seeing and hearing.

An example is from *An Officer and a Spy*, Robert Harris's historical thriller set in Paris in 1895. On page one, Major Picquart of the French army has been summoned to the residence of the Minister of War. In the lobby a young captain ushers Picquart.

> We march in step, the captain leading, over the black and white marble of the minister's official residence, up the curving staircase, past suits of silver armour from the time of Louis the Sun King, past that atrocious piece of Imperial kitsch, David's *Napoleon Crossing the Alps at the Col du Grand-Saint-Bernard*, until we reach the first floor, where we halt beside a window overlooking the grounds and the captain goes off to announce my arrival, leaving me alone for a few moments to contemplate something rare and beautiful: a garden made silent by snow in the centre of a city on a winter's morning.

Notice how much we learn about Major Picquart. By the way we see him "contemplate something rare and beautiful" we know he is not an uneducated boor but a man of fine sensibilities. Furthermore, look at the phrase "that atrocious piece of Imperial kitsch." This small detail tells us that Picquart is an art connoisseur—in fact, an art snob. For the author, what matters is not the painting on the wall but how Picquart *sees* it, because how he sees it tells the reader volumes about *him*. The point is that setting is a highly efficient way to reveal character. Instead of the author muscling in a chunk of deadwood backstory about Picquart's liberal arts education, the man's vivid flash of opinion about the painting says it all. This is the very essence of "Show, don't tell," and a fine example of how setting can do double duty: render setting *and* reveal character.

Here's another example of using attitude about a setting to reveal character. It's in Tami Hoag's thriller *The Bitter Season*, in a scene that comes within a few pages of the book's opening. It's rendered from the point of view of police officer Nikki Liska, the book's protagonist. She, two other officers, and the chief assistant county attorney are discussing a cold case:

> They sat at a round white melamine table in a war room commandeered from Homicide. Round tables were supposed to foster feelings of equality and cooperation, according to the industrial and psychological expert the department had wasted taxpayer dollars on during the last remodelling of the offices. The same expert had recommended painting the office walls mauve, and had told them they needed to remove the U bolts from the walls, so they had nowhere to cuff violent offenders if the need arose, because the threat of physical restraint might be deemed 'intimidating.' Weeks later a suspect had yanked a useless decorative shelf off the wall of an interview room and cracked Kovac in the head with it. He still had a little scar. Nikki had kneecapped the suspect with her tactical baton

before he could do worse. Thank God Kovac had
a head like granite.

Note how this little paragraph about setting, coming very
early in the book, does *triple* duty: it tells the setting, it gives
Nikki's attitude ("wasting taxpayer dollars"), and it shows that
Nikki can physically, even violently, take care of herself and her
partner, Kovac.

Reinforcing the "show, don't tell" principle, the most effective way to render setting is with action. Here is the opening of
Larry McMurtry's Pulitzer Prize-winning novel *Lonesome Dove*.

When Augustus came out on the porch the blue
pigs were eating a rattlesnake—not a very big
one. It had probably just been crawling around
looking for shade when it ran into the pigs. They
were having a fine tug-of-war with it, and its
rattling days were over. The sow had it by the
neck, and the shoat had the tail.

"You pigs git," Augustus said, kicking the
shoat. "Head on down to the creek if you want
to eat that snake." It was the porch he begrudged
them, not the snake. Pigs on the porch just
made things hotter, and things were already hot
enough. He stepped down into the dusty yard
and walked around to the springhouse to get his
jug. The sun was still high, sulled in the sky like
a mule, but Augustus had a keen eye for sun,
and to his eye the long light from the west had
taken on an encouraging slant.

> Evening took a long time getting to Lonesome Dove, but when it came it was a comfort. For most of the hours of the day—and most of the months of the year—the sun had the town trapped deep in dust, far out on the chaparral flats, a heaven for snakes and horned toads, roadrunners and stinging lizards, but a hell for pigs and Tennesseans.

McMurtry gives us the setting (a hot, parched, backwater town) by having Augustus deal with pigs tussling over a snake in the dust. He kicks a pig, though without malice, gets his jug, and gauges the slant of the sun. These are not big acts, just enough to "show" the setting with action rather than "tell" it with a mere neutral description of landscape. And, once again, the action does double duty of rendering setting and revealing something about Gus, a man wry, experienced, and self-assured.

Always, action is king.

CHAPTER 8

THE LITERARY LENS

"We know style when we see it. It's as effortless as Astaire's dancing, as appropriate as black at a funeral, as organic as a mulch-grown tomato."

CAROLYN WHEAT

MASTERING POINT OF VIEW

Who is telling your story? You, the writer, of course, but whose eyes do we see it through? One character? Two? Several? In making these choices you're using the technique called Point of View, often written as POV.

An analogy is in film, the placement of the camera in shooting a movie. The director and cinematographer must decide, shot by shot, how the camera "sees." Some shots will be depicted through one character's eyes, other shots through another character's eyes, and some will be shown through a neutral "eye in the sky." For writers of fiction, POV means this: as the story unfolds, which character is it told through? For inexperienced writers, it's trickier to master than it sounds. Orson Scott Card wrote an entire book on the subject, called *Characters and Viewpoint*, and it's a good one, complete with diagrams. Here, I'll distil the topic down to its essentials to help you make informed choices about POV that will suit the requirements of your particular story.

There are three common POV choices, used by the vast majority of novels:

- first person
- third person multiple, called omniscient
- third person limited

First person POV means the story is told through the voice of someone speaking about himself or herself: "I" and "me." The first sentence of *David Copperfield* by Charles Dickens is, "Whether I shall turn out to be the hero of my own life, or whether this station will be held by anybody else, these pages must show." That's first person.

Third person multiple/omniscient means that the author refers to characters by third person pronouns—"he" and "she" and "they"—and reveals any or all of the characters' thoughts and feelings. Omniscient means "all knowing," much like a god, and with this POV choice the narrator can move with god-like omnipresence through multiple locations, as if floating over the landscape, and dip into many characters' minds. Often, too, an omniscient narrator has a distinctly opinionated voice, commenting with a god-like authority on any subject that strikes her fancy: politics, architecture, orphanages, the American Civil

War, virtually anything. In *Moby-Dick*, Herman Melville gives extensive comments on whaling.

Third person limited means that, again, the author refers to characters using third person pronouns, but restricts the narrative to one point-of-view character or, at most, to just a few, which is why it's called limited. It's also limited in that there's little sense of the author's presence or opinions; the author remains invisible. We get deep inside the thoughts and feelings (what I call the head and heart) of the point-of-view character.

Each of these three common POV styles—first person, limited third person, and omniscient—has its advantages and drawbacks.

FIRST PERSON POV

The wonderful advantage of first person POV is that it's so direct, intimate, and immediate. As the reader, you feel you're physically in the presence of the person telling you their story, as if they are standing right in front of you. That can be exhilarating.

Another huge advantage is the opportunity it gives you to use, in the character's voice, their distinctive vocabulary, syntax, and idioms. Here are two sentences, each one from the POV of a child living in the second half of the nineteenth century, yet their voices are utterly different, born from vastly different lives:

- Mark Twain's Tom Sawyer: "You don't know about me without you have read a book by the name of The Adventures of Tom Sawyer; but that ain't no matter."
- Charlotte Bronte's Jane Eyre: "I cannot tell you what sentiment haunted the quite solitary churchyard with its inscribed tombstone; its gate, its two trees, its low

horizon, girdled by a broken wall and its newly risen crescent, attesting the hour of eventide."

Here are two longer examples that display this marvelous individuality of voice. The first is the opening paragraph of Nelson DeMille's thriller *Plum Island*. Look how DeMille depicts his protagonist, a wry street-smart cop, through first-person POV that is pitch perfect.

> Through my binoculars I could see this nice forty-something-foot cabin cruiser anchored a few hundred yards offshore. There were two thir-tyish couples aboard having a merry old time, banging down brews and whatever. The women had on teensy-weensy little bottoms and no tops, and one of the guys was standing on the bow and he slipped off his trunks and stood there a minute hanging hog, then jumped in the bay and swam around the boat. What a great country. I put down my binoculars and popped another Budweiser.

The first-person narrator's distinctive word choices—"banging down brews", "teensy-weensy", "hanging hog", "popped"—fairly grin with his personality.

The second example features a character whose voice is very different from the laid-back cop above. This one is French army officer Georges Picquart, the disciplined and intellectual pro-tagonist of Robert Harris's *An Officer and a Spy*. The novel is set in Paris in 1895 during the infamous, and true, miscarriage of justice in which Alfred Drefyus was convicted of treason and sent to the horrific Devil's Island prison. In this excerpt, three-quarters into the book, Picquart has been put on probation by the General Staff for having dared to question their charges against Dreyfus and initiating his own investigation. He knows his career is in jeopardy.

My uniform hangs in my wardrobe, like the sloughed-off skin of some former life. I have not been formally discharged from the army. Technically I am on indefinite leave pending the verdict of Pellieux's inquiry and the minister's response. But I prefer to dress in civilian clothes in order not to draw attention to myself. I put on a good stout overcoat and a bowler hat, take my umbrella from the stand and go out into the day.

Outwardly, I hope I wear my usual mask of detachment, even irony, for there has never been a situation, however dire, even this one, that did not strike me as containing at least some element of the human comedy. But then I think of Pauline, of how when I discovered her on my bed she could only keep repeating the same phrase, over and over: "He won't let me see the girls…" She has given a deposition to Pellieux and has fled the press and gone to stay with her brother, a naval officer, and her sister-in-law near Toulon. Louis has agreed to handle her legal affairs. He has advised us not to have any contact until the divorce is finalized. We said goodbye in a rainstorm in the Bois de Boulogne, watched by a sergeant of the Sûreté. And it is for what they have done to her, more even than what they have done to Dreyfus, that I cannot forgive the General Staff. For the first time in my life I carry hatred inside me. It is almost a physical thing, like a concealed knife. Sometimes, when I am alone, I like to take it out and run my thumb along its cold, sharp blade.

As you can see from the above examples, first person POV is thrillingly personal and intimate.

However, there are drawbacks to using first person narration. Here are three:

#1. It's restricting. The protagonist — the "I" — is the *only* character the reader gets to know intimately. All other characters are seen through that person's eyes. This means that the reader often can't connect with other characters on the same intense emotional level.

#2. The narrator must be present in every scene. This can cause plotting headaches. It can force the author into using clunky devices to move the plot forward, such as the narrator eavesdropping on other characters who reveal plot details through their dialogue. It can work, but it's clumsy.

#3. It can lead to "POV slip." Writers who aren't in control of first-person POV sometimes slip into the error of having the narrator state what another character thinks or feels, which is impossible; they can only *assume* what another person thinks and feels. Let's say your character is in a scene with his sister and we read: "She looked at me and she felt so angry about all the times she'd lost out on our mother's love." You've strained your reader's credulity, because the viewpoint character cannot possibly *know* what his sister feels, he can only speculate.

THIRD PERSON MULTIPLE/ OMNISCIENT POV

When the author uses an omniscient POV the reader accepts the narrator's god-like knowledge of every character's inner life. The author/narrator floats above the story, dipping in and out of multiple characters' thoughts whenever necessary. The great strength of the omniscient POV lies in depicting a panoramic cast of characters. It was commonly used in the "large canvas" novels of the nineteenth century, such as the works of Dickens and Tolstoy.

Today, it's much less common. Some writers still use it to excellent effect, such as Vikram Seth in *A Suitable Boy* and John Irving in his books like *A Widow For One Year*. But, in general, the POV of omniscience has an old-fashioned feel, because it can have a distancing effect on the reader. Here's why. As the omniscient narrator moves in and out of a dozen or more characters' minds, the reader is kept from fully engaging with *any* of them. We don't get truly, deeply inside any individual's head or heart because the narrator is always there, above it all, aloof, telling us how to view them. Here's an example, an excerpt, slightly abridged, from Ian McEwan's *Atonement*. I'm taking great license here, because this brilliant novel is a highly skillful blend of omniscient POV and limited third person POV, but this particular passage is omniscient, so it makes my point.

In Leon's life, or rather, in his account of his life, no one was mean-spirited, no one schemed or lied or betrayed. Everyone was celebrated at least in some degree ... He remembered all his friends' best lines. The effect of one of Leon's anecdotes was to make his listener warm to humankind and its failings. Everyone was, at a minimal estimate, a "good egg" or "a decent sort," and motivation was never judged to be at variance with outward show. If there was mystery or contradiction in a friend, Leon took the long view and found a benign explanation. Literature and politics, science and religion did not bore him – they simply had no place in his world, and nor did any matter about which people seriously disagreed. He had taken a degree in law and was happy to have forgotten the whole experience. It was hard to imagine him ever lonely, or bored or despondent; his equanimity was bottomless, as was his lack of ambition, and he assumed that everyone else was much like him. Despite all this, his blandness was perfectly tolerable, even soothing.

In that passage, the reader sees Leon very clearly, which is wonderful—it's even fun—but we also know we're not getting Leon's description of himself. It's obviously the author telling us these things, because no character, no person, would ever think of himself in such terms. We're not inside Leon's head, experiencing his thoughts, we're on the outside looking in. We're spectators, being *told* how to think about him. So, with omniscient narration, instead of the reader living a character's frustration or bafflement or joy or anguish along *with* them, we're made to take a distant, almost ironic stance, watching what the character does but not experiencing it. That weakens the emotional connection between characters and the reader. A less emotional experience is a less powerful experience.

THIRD PERSON LIMITED POV

Lying between the narrow restrictions of first person POV and the broad detachment of omniscient narration is the fertile ground of third person limited POV. It is overwhelmingly the popular choice for most novels today.

With limited third person POV the author delves deeply into just a very *few* characters' hearts and minds—their hopes and fears and desires—one character at a time. All the other characters are seen through their eyes. Commonly with this POV technique, each viewpoint character gets a whole scene or even a whole chapter rendered through their voice alone, moving the story forward through their actions. By laying bare these select characters' feelings, the author establishes a tight emotional bond between the character and the reader. We relate richly to these characters. Just as important, the author doesn't intrude with editorial commentary; the author remains virtually invisible.

In the hands of a skilled writer, third person limited POV can feel just as direct and intimate as first person. Here's an example from Kate Atkinson's novel *Started Early, Took My Dog.* This paragraph, slightly abbreviated, features Tracy Waterhouse, a big-boned British police constable who's fortyish and single. Her thoughts and feelings are so personal, so individual, she *seems* to be talking to us in the first person. In this passage she

has just come out of a sweets shop "stuffing her forage" into her
shoulder bag.

> Viennese truffles, her midweek treat. Pathetic
> really. Other people went to the cinema on an
> evening, to restaurants, pubs and clubs, visited
> friends, had sex, but Tracy was looking forward
> to curling up on her sofa with *Britain's Got Talent*
> and a bag of Thornton's Viennese truffles. When
> had she last eaten a meal with someone in a
> restaurant? That bloke from the dating agency,
> a couple of year ago, in Dino's in Bishopsgate?
> She could remember what she'd eaten—garlic
> bread, spaghetti and meatballs, followed by a
> crème caramel—yet she couldn't recall the bloke's
> name. "You're a big girl," he'd said when she met
> him for a drink beforehand in Whitelock's.
> "Yeah," she said. "Want to make something
> of it?" Downhill from there on really.

Here's another example, this one from the opening of
Stephen King's *The Girl Who Loved Tom Gordon*. King makes
this little girl's voice so real, so ineffably *her*, it's hard to imagine
that first person narration could make it any more intimate.
Here's page one:

> The world had teeth and it could bite you with
> them any time it wanted. Trisha McFarland
> discovered this when she was nine years old. At
> ten o'clock on a morning in early June she was

sitting in the back of her mother's Dodge caravan, wearing her blue Red Sox batting practice
jersey (the one with 36 Gordon on the back), and
playing with Mona, her doll. At ten-thirty she
was lost in the woods. By eleven she was trying
not to be terrified, trying not to think, *This is
serious, this is very serious.* Trying not to think
that sometimes when people got lost in the woods
they got seriously hurt. Sometimes they died.

All because I needed to pee, she thought.
Except she hadn't needed to pee all that badly.
And in any case she could have asked Mom and
Pete to wait up the trail a minute while she went
behind a tree. They were fighting again, gosh
what a surprise *that* was, and that's why she had
dropped behind a little bit, and without saying
anything. That was why she had stepped off the
trail and behind a high stand of bushes. She
needed a breather, simple as that.

If you're using third person limited POV I recommend that
you do, indeed, *limit* it: stick to about three or four point-of-
view characters. More than that can make the reader start to
wonder: whose story is this? Naturally, you can *show* many more
characters, but they'll all be seen through the eyes of one of your
viewpoint characters. It's a matter of emphasis.

> Focusing on a limited number of
> POV characters delivers the greatest
> emotional impact.

How do you chose which character will be a scene's viewpoint character? Author Elmore Leonard says he chooses the one who best "brings the scene to life." Here's my recommendation:

> In any scene, make the POV character the one who has the most at stake, materially or emotionally.

POV VARIATIONS

The POV techniques above are the three most common, but writers have created some very sophisticated variations. Let's look at five.

Variation #1. More than one first-person narrator.

In *The Poisonwood Bible,* Barbara Kingsolver gives us five different first-person narrators. They're all members of an American Baptist missionary family stationed in the former Belgian Congo during that colony's fight for independence. The four daughters (Rachel, Leah, Adah, and Ruth May) and their mother Orleanna each get rotating chapters all to themselves, and Kingsolver states in each chapter heading which of them is narrating it. The book is a marvel of style, with each first person viewpoint rendered in a wholly distinct voice.

Variation #2. The unreliable narrator.

Ford Maddox Ford used this device in *The Good Soldier.* The reader gradually comes to understand that the narrator, telling us about the story's criss-crossing love affairs, is deeply involved in these affairs and also hasn't exactly given us the unvarnished truth. In Anthony Burgess's dystopian *A Clockwork Orange,* readers soon realize they can't completely trust anything the manipulative sociopath Alex tells us. In John Grisham's *The Racketeer,* the narrator, jailed lawyer Malcolm Bannister, is a first-person narrator with a clever plan, but for most of the novel he's very sly in withholding from the reader the *whole* truth about what he's up to.

Variation #3. The first-person narrator telling someone else's story.

Joseph Conrad did this in *Lord Jim,* having Marlowe tell Jim's story. Arthur Conan Doyle famously used this technique in his Sherlock Holmes novels in which Doctor Watson, speaking in the first person, tells about his friend Holmes and the cases they work on. I suspect Doyle felt readers might find it hard to identify with the arrogant, unapproachable, drug-addicted Holmes, whereas it's easy for us to identify with the friendly "everyman" Doctor Watson. A more recent example is the first person narrator in Robert Harris's trio of novels set in ancient Rome that feature the wily orator-politician Cicero. We experience Cicero's plottings, relationships, triumphs, and defeats, yet the narrator throughout is his secretary, his accomplished slave Tiro.

Variation #4. Letters and diaries.

By using letters or entries in a diary an author can reap the power of a first person voice inside a story rendered in another POV. One of English literature's first novels, Samuel Richardson's *Clarissa,* published in 1748, unfolds through an intricate web of letters, including those of Clarissa Harlowe, a young woman of high principles and deep humanity, and of

Robert Lovelace, who attracts her and then ruins her, a man dubbed by the critic Robert McCrum as "the most charming villain in English literature." The book is composed solely of letters, yet it has great power. McCrum calls it "a novel with the simplicity of myth."

In our own time two highly skilled writers have used this technique to augment their third-person narratives. Gillian Flynn's bestselling psychological thriller *Gone Girl* gives us the high-strung, scheming Amy through her intense entries in her journal. And A.S. Byatt, in her award-winning novel *Possession*, develops some of her intricate plot via love letters exchanged by two Victorian poets.

Variation #5. A mix of first person and third person.

This technique used to be rare but is becoming slightly more common. In *The Racketeer* John Grisham intercuts sequences of the first person voice of incarcerated lawyer Malcolm Bannister, the protagonist, with third person sequences of various characters during FBI interrogations.

All of these variation techniques can work to great effect. However, if you're writing your first novel, I recommend choosing one of the two most common POV methods—first person or third person limited—and sticking with it throughout your story. Experiment in a later book, once you have the technique well under control.

CINEMATIC DISTANCE

The distance the reader feels between himself or herself and the events in the story can, and does, constantly shift. Think of a movie with the camera sometimes viewing scenes from afar, at other times moving in for a medium shot, then a close-up, and sometimes an extreme close-up. Each of these cinematic choices produces a particular effect, ranging from detachment to intensity—emotionally, from cool to warmer to hot. Referring to the same phenomenon in fiction, John Gardner uses the phrase "psychic distance" in his book *The Art of Fiction*. By manipulating psychic distance, the novelist achieves the same effects as a film does. Mastering this tool of writing craft, much like POV, is not easy. So it's helpful to take a close look at how to handle the technique.

Compare the following five brief paragraphs. Number 1 establishes a cinematic/psychic distance that is long: the reader is far away from the subject. Number 2 moves in slightly, and so on, until in example Number 5 the cinematic/psychic distance is virtually nonexistent.

1. *"It was a summer day in 2016. A woman left her house and walked to her car. A year ago she had been in a highway accident."*

   The reader is viewing this from far away. The feeling is detached, formal in presentation, emotionally cool.

2. *"Jane Dougherty was anxious about driving again. The accident had happened just ten months ago."*

   Less distance. Less detachment.

3. *"Jane hated the thought of getting behind the wheel again. The accident had broken her arm in two places. Hard to forget."*

   Moving in closer. Warmer emotionally.

4. *"God, she hated getting behind the wheel. Hated remembering her own screams and the blood and the stench of burning rubber."*
A close-up. More intense. Getting hotter emotionally.

5. *"Do it. Key in ignition. Hands on wheel. Forget the arm, the jabbing pain. Forget the fear. Drive."*
Extreme close-up. Extreme intensity. Emotionally hot.

When an inexperienced writers uses sudden and inexplicable shifts in cinematic/psychic distance it looks amateurish, and tends to push the reader away. For example, notice the sudden shifts in this short paragraph:

> Peter Horton hated snakes. Christ, he thought, they make me puke. The young man had never known any snakes personally, but Pete knew what he felt.

These three sentences lurch from distance ("Peter Horton hated snakes") to a hyper-personal, extreme close-up ("Christ, he thought, they make me puke") then jerk us back out to extreme distance ("The young man had never known any snakes personally") then in again to mid-distance ("but Pete knew how he felt"). As readers, we reel in and out so abruptly it almost makes us seasick. If this were a series of four film shots they would start with a wide shot, zoom in to a sudden close-up of a horrified pair of eyes, instantly pull back to a wide shot, then zoom back in on Pete's face. A viewer might, indeed, feel their lunch backing up.

A skilled writer carefully controls the shifts in cinematic/psychic distance. The beginning of a story usually depicts an event in either long or medium distance. (In filmmaking this is called a series of "establishing shots.") Later, the writer moves closer into a scene, providing more intensity, then draws back slightly for smooth transitions, and then, at a scene's turning point, might move in still closer for extreme intensity. Variations of all kinds are possible, but the sequences must be carefully composed, just as a cinematographer would compose shots throughout a scene.

Here are two examples of skillful manipulation of this technique. The first is the opening of Stephen King's *The Girl Who Loved Tom Gordon*. (It's the same passage given above in the section on Point of View.) Note how the first two sentences have us looking at the character from afar, with a wide shot, starting with the opening phrase "The world had teeth" and by giving us a character's full name: "Trisha McFarland." (A full name always occurs only in a wide shot, since no character *thinks* of herself or himself as first-name-and-last-name, except perhaps a megalomaniac.) Then King moves in closer, slowly, into medium shots. He finesses this transition with a list of specific details (the Dodge caravan, the blue Red Sox jersey, the doll Mona) making us feel nearer to Trisha—near enough, in fact, to read the number on her jersey—and then to her being "lost in the woods." Then, the words in italics (*This is serious, this is very serious*) shorten the cinematic/psychic distance still more, giving us Trish's intense thoughts—a close-up—so that as we roll into the second paragraph this close-up on her continues.

> The world had teeth and it could bite you with
> them any time it wanted. Trisha McFarland

discovered this when she was nine years old. At ten o'clock on a morning in early June she was sitting in the back of her mother's Dodge caravan, wearing her blue Red Sox batting practice jersey (the one with 36 Gordon on the back), and playing with Mona, her doll. At ten-thirty she was lost in the woods. By eleven she was trying not to be terrified, trying not to think, *This is serious, this is very serious.* Trying not to think that sometimes when people got lost in the woods they got seriously hurt. Sometimes they died.

All because I needed to pee, she thought. Except she hadn't needed to pee all that badly. And in any case she could have asked Mom and Pete to wait up the trail a minute while she went behind a tree. They were fighting again, gosh what a surprise *that* was, and that's why she had dropped behind a little bit, and without saying anything. That was why she had stepped off the trail and behind a high stand of bushes. She needed a breather, simple as that.

Larry McMurtry, too, carefully controls the variations in cinematic/psychic distance in the opening three paragraphs of *Lonesome Dove*, his sweeping Western that won the Pulitzer Prize. But McMurtry's technique is slightly different than the one King uses in the passage above. Instead of opening with a wide shot, *Lonesome Dove* opens with two paragraphs of medium shots. We're a medium psychic distance from Augustus as we get his personal view of the critters he's watching; though it's personal, it's not yet a close-up. Then, for the third paragraph, the "camera" pulls back, greatly widening the shot—and the psychic distance—by giving emotionally cool comments on the town in its doldrums of heat.

> When Augustus came out on the porch the blue pigs were eating a rattlesnake—not a very big one. It had probably just been crawling around looking for shade when it ran into the pigs. They were having a fine tug-of-war with it, and its rattling days were over. The sow had it by the neck, and the shoat had the tail.
>
> "You pigs git," Augustus said, kicking the shoat. "Head on down to the creek if you want to eat that snake." It was the porch he begrudged them, not the snake. Pigs on the porch just made things hotter, and things were already hot enough. He stepped down into the dusty yard and walked around to the springhouse to get his jug. The sun was still high, sulled in the sky like a mule, but Augustus had a keen eye for sun, and to his eye the long light from the west had taken on an encouraging slant.
>
> Evening took a long time getting to Lonesome Dove, but when it came it was a comfort. For most of the hours of the day—and most of the months of the year—the sun had the town trapped deep in dust, far out on the chaparral flats, a heaven for snakes and horned

toads, roadrunners and stinging lizards, but a
hell for pigs and Tennesseans.

Study other fine writing like this and note how accomplished
authors manipulate cinematic/psychic distance in order to manipulate the reader's emotional "temperature," and thus deliver
the richest experience. Readers crave an emotional bond with
characters. It's the soul of the page-turner.

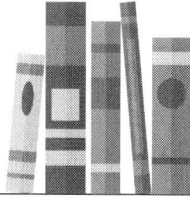

PART IV

THE BUSINESS

CHAPTER 9

GETTING PUBLISHED

*"Literature is like any other trade; you will never
sell anything unless you go to the right shop."*
GEORGE BERNARD SHAW

TRUTHS ABOUT THE INDUSTRY

If you're an emerging writer hoping to sign with a literary agent
and get your book published by a major publishing house, the
publishing industry can seem like a bewildering, even impen-
etrable, labyrinth. A cacophony of warnings, rules, guidelines,
and do's and don'ts about how to break into the business shout at
the writer from social media platforms, in blogs, and at writers'
conferences and pitch fests. It can leave a writer feeling frustrated
and even intimidated.

Here's the good news. Publishers are *always* looking for
wonderful new novels. They long to find that undiscovered gem

of a manuscript, and to be the champion who unveils it to the world. The same holds true for agents. Junior agents are eager to sign new writers, because they need to build their list of clients whose books they can sell, and even top agents with a lucrative roster of established and bestselling clients are always open to a manuscript that's extraordinary. The truth is, nothing makes all of these industry professionals happier than to discover exciting new talent. It's a personal thrill for them, because they sincerely love books. It's also a sweet boost for their careers. Finding and selling wonderful books is what agents and publishers are in business for.

But here's another truth. All of these pros—agents, and acquisition editors at publishing houses—are deluged with manuscripts that range from awful to commonplace. They read submissions constantly—every day and most nights, including weekends—and the vast majority of the material does not rise above mediocrity. They read so much that, sometimes, during a late night read, a manuscript that can simply pass the test of "not awful" can strike a hopeful spark. One former agent calls it "standards creep." But the spark is snuffed out when harsh morning light exposes the story, after all, as derivative, predictable, or peopled with lacklustre characters.

And then there are other times (sadly, quite frequent) when the agent or editor comes across a manuscript they really like—it's fresh and lively and it touches them—but, again, that cold morning light is brutal, and it forces this professional to conclude that, much as they might *wish* they could take on the book, they don't think there's a big enough market for it—perhaps it has too narrow a target audience, or perhaps its topic fits a trend that is waning, or perhaps the opposite, a topic so startling they sense the world may not yet be ready for it—so they just can't get behind it. They would be the first to admit they are not infallible about marketability; nevertheless, they have to *feel* that a book could be a winner. They have to fall in love with it. Because the commitment to taking on a book is huge. An agent can spend months, even years, "shopping" a novel before finding a publisher for it. As for an editor at a publishing house, she must make an equal commitment, because she has to be the book's champion within her firm and do battle, sometimes, with other departments who doubt the book can succeed. When this happens—when an agent or editor wishes they could take on a book but just can't see a way to get behind it—it truly breaks their heart to say no to the writer.

For the writer, of course, this can be devastating. But that doesn't change the marketplace reality, which is that agents and publishing house editors work in a business, not a literary admiration society. They have to sell books to the public, lots of books. If they don't, they get fired.

An emerging writer's best chance for success lies in writing a book that is both compelling *and* marketable.

All the lessons in the previous chapters will help you create a compelling story. Now, it's time to emphasize the importance of making it marketable. I'll start with an examination of genre. Following it, you'll find specifics on how to submit your manuscript to agents and publishers.

The World of Genres

Most novels that are page-turners fall into a half-dozen main categories called genres: romance, mystery, thriller, science fiction, fantasy, and horror. Of these, the biggest selling genres are the first three. Novels that do not fit any genre are called mainstream fiction.

Genre matters to publishers, because they have a better chance of selling a book when readers knows the book's category: there's a proven market. It's also the likeliest way for a writer to break into the business. Agents, publishers, book stores, and online booksellers live in a constant storm of marketing noise, and almost all the noise is about books by bankable, star authors. If your book cannot be categorized, it will not be heard above this noise.

Genres developed over the centuries as a classification system for dramas. Aristotle started the tradition, delineating four types of drama based on whether a play had a major reversal, which he called a complex plot, or whether it didn't, which he called a simple plot, and also based on the type of ending. In the centuries since then, scholars have developed other systems, categorizing by story structure and story values. It can be argued that all novels, no matter how "literary," fall within the bounds of some genre. Jane Austen's *Pride and Prejudice* is a romance. Dostoevsky's *Crime and Punishment* is a psychological thriller. Mary Shelley's *Frankenstein* is horror. Jules Verne's *Twenty Thousand Leagues Under the Sea* is science fiction. Today, film dominates our culture, and screenwriters are adept at classifying their work within a whole suite of genres, including love story, war story, coming of age, western, social drama, crime, action, detective, mockumentary, courtroom drama, epic, myth, heist, adventure, and comedy ranging from satire to farce. In Hollywood, this categorization is called "positioning." Positioning the audience is an age-old practice. Shakespeare didn't call his play *Hamlet*, he called it *The Tragedy of Hamlet, Prince of Denmark*, and he gave his comedies titles like *All's Well That Ends Well* and *Much Ado About Nothing* and *The Merry Wives of Windsor*, so when audiences entered the Globe Theatre every afternoon, the plays' titles psychologically primed them to cry or laugh.

Today, for the very same reasons, categorizing novels into genres has become a marketing imperative. Booksellers want genres in order to know which shelf to put a book on, even a website "shelf." Publishers' sales reps need genres because they get only a few minutes to pitch new titles to chain bookstore buyers. Agents need genres to pitch your book efficiently to publishers. Classifying novels by genre is a fact of life in the publishing industry. So it's helpful to understand what "genre" is, and what it isn't.

Each genre imposes conventions on story design. For example, in a romance there must be these three acts: girl meets boy, girl loses boy, girl gets boy. In a mystery, there must be a dead body, an investigation, and the revelation of the murderer. In a thriller there must be suspense and danger, with such conventions as a high-stakes hunt, a looming fatal deadline, and the hero taking a big personal risk that finally defeats the antagonist. Readers know these conventions and expect to see them fulfilled.

But don't misunderstand: conventions are not clichés. A cliché is the same old situation used to fulfill the convention. But there can be breathtakingly fresh ways to fulfill the convention. Scott Turow's mystery *Presumed Innocent* broke new ground in 1987 for its psychological depth and literary verve, and it spent forty-five weeks on The New York Times bestseller list. Turow fulfills the convention of the investigation by making the narrator-protagonist, Rusty Sabich, the prosecutor handling the murder case: he must find the killer and bring that person to justice. But there's no cliché as Rusty, who had an affair with the dead woman, becomes the suspect and is arrested, and only at the climax does he discover that the killer is … *(No spoilers here. Enjoy the book!)*

Readers want conventions, but they also want their expectations reversed. They like a story that gives an insight they never saw coming. "Insight" means literally seeing the truth through and under the surface of things. A genre novel can push the conventions to the limit, revealing deep truths about our humanity, and when that happens storytelling becomes art. For example, critics and millions of readers alike agree that John LeCarré's novels such as *A Most Wanted Man* transcend the thriller genre. Yet they are easily identified as thrillers.

Some emerging writers don't like having their work categorized; they prefer to call it literary fiction. There are no hard rules about what separates literary fiction from popular/commercial fiction (genre fiction), and there's a great deal of overlap, like the works of John LeCarré. However, in broad terms, I would differentiate the two by these five criteria:

1. *Action.* In popular/commercial fiction the protagonist is pro-active; he or she is actively seeking something, actively dealing with conflict. In literary fiction the protagonist is often more passive and introspective.

2. *Conflict.* In popular fiction the protagonist struggles against primarily *external* forces of conflict: other people. The literary protagonist often faces mostly *internal* conflict: himself/herself.

3. *Causality.* In popular fiction the world is a place of cause and effect: characters take actions that have meaningful results. This expresses the *connectedness* of life. In literary fiction, randomness often rules the universe, expressing the *disconnectedness* of life, the sense that people have little control over the haphazard nature of existence.

4. *Language.* In popular fiction all that's necessary in style and language is clarity, what George Orwell called "windowpane" prose. Literary fiction focuses on artistic language. The aura of poetry is the hallmark of a literary novel.

5. *Closure.* In popular fiction closure is essential—that is, at the end there's a meaningful resolution to the protagonist's struggle. Literary endings are often open-ended, sometimes even ambiguous.

Literary fiction does not sell well. The further a writer moves away from a straightforward story featuring an active protagonist struggling against external forces, to an ambiguous story with a passive, introspective protagonist, the more their potential readership shrinks. Agents and publishers are keenly aware of this bottom line. When an agent or an acquisition editor at a publishing house reads a query in which the writer refers to their manuscript as a literary novel, that industry professional translates it in their mind as *Won't sell more than five thousand copies.* If you're sure your manuscript fits no genre, it's wiser to call it mainstream fiction.

Writing in a popular genre will not restrict your creativity. Each genre can be rich with themes, and each deals with crucial human values: love and hate, war and peace, justice and injustice, achievement and failure.

Also, within each genre are many sub-genres. For example, regarding thrillers there are the spy thrillers of John LeCarré, the legal thrillers of John Grisham, the psychological thrillers of Gillian Flynn and Denis Lehane and Joy Fielding, the techno-thrillers of Tom Clancy. In mysteries, the subgenres range from the ever-popular cozy (the publishing industry's term for a murder story in a small community of basically nice people, with the violence happening offstage) to the gritty, gory offerings of a police procedural, with many sub-categories in between, including (to name just a few): caper, noir, historical, amateur sleuth, professional sleuth, comic, and child-in-peril. For romance, the sub-genres seem endless, including historical romance, romantic suspense, romantic comedy, chick-lit, young adult, erotica, Christian, paranormal, sweet (a romance centered on a virgin heroine and a storyline containing little or no sex), and spicy (a romance in which married characters work to resolve their problems).

Superb books have been written in each genre. And popular fiction, from the work of Charles Dickens to that of Harper Lee, can explore important issues about our world. With *To Kill a Mockingbird*, Harper Lee didn't write a literary rumination on racism. She wrote a popular story about people in crisis, complete with a courtroom drama.

Deep Genre

Thrillers happen to be a genre I write in (contemporary thrillers and historical thrillers) so I've given much thought to this particular territory. It's often said that a good thriller is like a roller-coaster ride. That's true enough. The genre is about high stakes, countdowns, and suspense, and every compelling thriller delivers this kind of excitement. But the most satisfying thrillers deliver more: an exciting story that also explores complex issues. This kind of story has something important to say about our world. It takes the reader away from the amusement park and sends them on a voyage, an exhilarating journey into a different way of thinking. I call it Deep Genre.

Popular fiction is one of the best ways to illuminate crucial issues of our time, because we see those issues brought to life by characters we care deeply about, characters thrown into terrible dilemmas where they are forced to take risks and make hard choices. Characters who bring us face-to-face with the gripping question: *If I were in that situation, what would I do?* That's the job of Deep Genre.

We're all familiar with the conventions of the genre as a roller-coaster ride. The life-and-death stakes. The antagonist making the stakes personal for the hero. The hero at the mercy of the villain, then turning the tables and coming out on top. The false ending. Effective tropes, all. However, a Deep Genre thriller takes readers beyond their expectations. It cracks open their comfort zone and gives them an insight they never saw coming. "Insight" means seeing the truth through the surface of things. It's the serious novelist's job to challenge not only readers' expectations, but also their received wisdom, their acceptance of society's status quo, especially regarding power. Deep Genre is often about fighting power.

Charles Dickens knew this when he used his immensely popular novels to hold a mirror up to the horrors that working-class people suffered under unfettered capitalism in nineteenth-century England. In our time, bestselling author John Grisham has often done the same with his thrillers about the "little guy" up against some form of corporate bully. In *The Rainmaker* it's the powerful insurance industry; in *The Street Lawyer* it's mega-developers who force homeless people to their death. Like Dickens, Grisham uses Deep Genre to say what needs to be said.

Author James Scott Bell offers these words of wisdom: "The original storytellers spun thrillers. When heroes went out into the dark world to confront monsters and demons and great beasts, the tribe vicariously lived the tale. But there was something more—they learned how to fight, act courageously and survive. The first thrillers carried a message and helped bring a local community together."

Christopher Vogler echoes that truth in his book *The Writer's Journey*. His twelve-step layout of the "hero's journey" explores the shared elements that have animated powerful myths and fairy tales in all cultures, in all times. Following any story's climax, a dénouement is needed to bring the story to a meaningful conclusion, and Vogler says this final step of the hero's journey entails bringing back an "elixir," something that heals the rupture that originally incited the hero's perilous adventure. The elixir might be literal: food for the starving tribe, for example. In a big techno-thriller, it might even heal the world. Or it might be abstract: a hard-won wisdom that heals a shattered family. Whatever it is, if the hero does not bring back something to share, he remains unenlightened, adolescent. He hasn't grown. And, therefore, neither can the reader. In other words, the roller-coaster ride is all you get.

A brilliant Deep Genre thriller is Robert Harris's *An Officer and a Spy,* set in France in 1895. Georges Picquart is the real-life colonel in the French army who exposed the corrupt cabal of generals who'd sent an innocent man, Alfred Dreyfus, to rot in solitary confinement on Devil's Island. Picquart puts his career, and eventually his life, in jeopardy by seeking justice in the face of the army's massive cover-up. This story's tense conflict between state corruption and individual principle resonates in our time of "ordinary" people taking great personal risk to fight power, be it a dominant democracy's vast surveillance state or a totalitarian regime's oppression. John LeCarré gives us tragic Deep Genre in *A Most Wanted Man,* his raw response to the war on terror that has bleakened our world. As reviewer Hari Kunzru says, LeCarré portrays "the quiet ruthlessness of intelligence organisations, and the terror of the moment when an unsuspecting person drops through the trapdoor that separates the everyday world from the secret one."

A great thriller may end in tragedy, as does LeCarré's. Or the protagonist's struggle against power may end with justice prevailing, as does the tale of Harris's Colonel Picquart. Either way, readers welcome the experience. Because it's not the roller-coaster ride that satisfies the soul; it's the voyage. When the roller-coaster comes to a stop, you're back where you began. A voyage takes you some place new.

The same serious intent, and content, imbue fine novels of other genres too, whether romance, mystery, science fiction, or fantasy. My advice is to be honest in your choice of genre. Write the kind of story you like to read. Don't write something because friends think you should, and don't write in the hope of inspiring critical praise. That's a waste of your talent and time. Writing a novel is a marathon; it takes endurance. Unless you write what interests you, you'll give up without finishing the race. So write in the genre you love.

BREAKING IN

Let's say you've followed all the advice in this book, from creating a storyline, to writing several drafts of the novel, to getting an expert evaluation and revising the work using that professional's suggestions. You're confident that you've now produced a compelling and marketable manuscript: a page-turner. First, congratulate yourself. You've done what thousands say they want to do, but never actually do. You've written a book. Only those who've made it to "The End" understand the determination this requires.

Now you're all set to get the book published and send it out into the world. So, how do you do that?

There are two main routes that can take your book to market. The first is in partnership with a publisher, a firm that does what's called traditional publishing. Their employees supply editorial expertise, cover design, interior layout, production, printing, promotion, marketing, shipping, and distribution nation-wide to bookstore chains and other major retail outlets like Walmart and Costco, as well as online. The traditional publisher expends capital for all these services, then pays the writer a royalty on book sales. The second route is to self publish; you get your book out by publishing it independently. This chapter will look very briefly at self publishing, and then focus on traditional publishing.

Self publishing appeals to emerging writers because the royalty they earn on sales is much higher (for example, seventy percent for e-books sold by KDP on Amazon) than the standard royalty offered by publishers (often around ten percent for a hardcover book). However, the self published writer must personally arrange and pay for every step of the editorial and production process before offering the book for sale via online entities like Amazon. Furthermore, distribution of physical books by national bookstore chains, and by national retailers like Walmart and Costco, is rarely available to the independently published author. Because of this enormous distribution challenge, most writers who self publish sell a very limited number of their books. That puts a different slant on the royalty math.

The world of self publishing is rapidly evolving, and a detailed examination of its processes, benefits, and drawbacks is beyond the scope of this book. (There are dozens of books, websites, and blogs dedicated to the topic, all with valuable information.) Instead, we'll now look at the steps you need to take that lead to a traditional publisher.

So, how do you get your manuscript onto a publisher's desk? It breaks down into three processes:

- Formatting your manuscript correctly
- Writing the query letter
- Finding an agent

FORMATTING YOUR MANUSCRIPT

There are publishing industry standards for formatting a manuscript—font, spacing, indents, page numbering, etc.—and it's important to observe them. New writers often don't. They think: It's my book's *content* that matters, and once an agent or editor reads it they'll love it, so what difference does it make how the pages look?

It matters a lot. Imagine a lawyer thinking like that. She's so sure of her case, so prepared, so confident the judge will see the evidence her way, she arrives in court in track pants and a T-shirt. After all, she reasons, it's the *case* that matters and the judge knows that, so what difference does proper legal attire make? No lawyer would make this self-defeating mistake.

First impressions are crucial; you know how hard it is to change them. And the first impression a writer gets to make on an agent or an editor at a publishing house is the *look* of their manuscript: its formatting. Publishing industry professionals read manuscripts constantly and any inordinate irregularities— if, for example, the writer has used a strange font, or hasn't double-spaced the lines—will irritate them. They will see the writer as someone so ignorant, or defiant, or indifferent that he hasn't even made the effort to find out the industry standards. Their first impression will be a negative one. They know from experience that when a writer's presentation is careless, often the writing is too. You have enough obstacles to overcome in getting your book published, so don't let something as petty as formatting prevent you, and your book, from being taken seriously. As New York agent Noah Lukeman, says, "Your creativity should be expressed in your writing, not your font." Use this first chance to make a positive impression on the industry pro, with a perfectly formatted manuscript, and get them on your side.

Here are the guidelines you need.

Publishing Industry Standards for Formatting a Manuscript

- Double space all pages. The only exception is the title page (see below).
- Font: 12-point in Times New Roman, black. No odd fonts; no colored fonts.
- Indent every paragraph, including dialogue. Use the standard tab of .5 inch.
- Set the margins at 1 inch or 1.25 inches at the top, bottom, and both sides.
- Leave one double space between paragraphs, not two. (The only exception is to mark a break between sections or scenes; there, leave two double spaces.)
- Put no gimmicks such as drawings or designs anywhere on the manuscript.
- On the title page enter the contact information—author's name, address, phone number, and email address—in the upper left corner, single spaced. About half-way down the page, in the center, enter the title in capital letters. Leave one double-spaced line and enter "by" followed by the author's name either on the same line or one line below. Add the rough word count ("rough" means rounded up to the nearest hundred) in the upper right corner.
- Number the pages consecutively in the upper right corner. On every page *after* the title page (the title page is not numbered) enter the page number preceded by the author's surname, like this: Kyle/83. If you wish, add the title, or keywords from the title, like this: Kyle/The Queen's Captive/83.

- Begin each new chapter on a new page. Start the text about one third of the way down from the top of the page. If using a chapter heading, center it, then leave two double-spaced lines, then continue the text.
- On the final page, to mark the end of the manuscript, enter a number sign (#) on an otherwise blank line one double-spaced line below the final line of text. Or simply write *The End*. You want agents and editors to know they've reached the end.

If sending hard copy:
- Use standard 8.5 x 11 paper, 20-lb bond, white only (no colors), no high gloss.
- Print on one side of the page only.
- Leave the manuscript unbound: no covers, no clips, no three-hole punches—just the loose pages in a tidy stack. Secure it with an elastic if you wish.

The following example shows correct title page format and manuscript format.

Will Shakespeare
3 Witches Way
London, U.K.
SW1X 7AX
(071) 235-3333
thebard@theglobe.com

Author Information
12-point Times New Roman
Single Spaced

96,000 words

Word Count
Right Align

ROMEO AND ETHEL, THE PIRATE'S DAUGHTER

by

Will Shakespeare

Title
ALL CAPS,
half way down page

Margins
1 to 1.25"

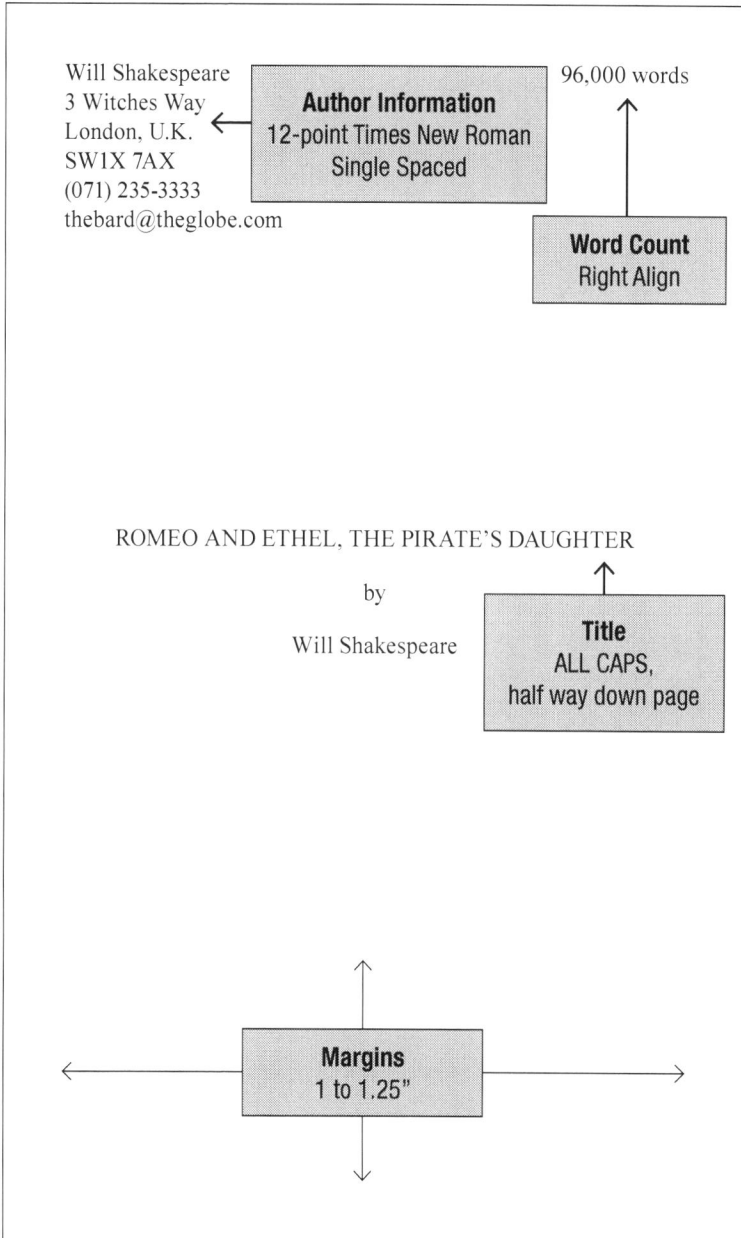

Example of correct title page format

Chapter
Start New Page
Begin a Third Down
Center Chapter Title
Follow w/ Double Space

→ **Chapter 6**

Honor wiped a trickle of sweat from her brow, her spade idle in her hands as she took in what Adam had just said. "A project?" she asked warily. "What kind of project?"

She was preparing the soil for transplanting some rose bushes to the borders of her herb garden. Dirty knobs of snow clung stubbornly to hollows in the earth, like vagrants claiming squatting rights, and despite the body warmth the work generated, the March wind chilled her nose and fingertips. She had allowed herself a few days at home before returning to Elizabeth at Woodstock, and in this brief time she longed to start things growing. The Princess was proving a frustratingly obstinate pupil, but of *this* endeavor—tending her flowers and her herb garden—Honor was master.

But Adam's news was serious. To steady her spade, Honor jammed it into the garden loam. That shot a pain to her rib that made her wince.

"Here, let me," he said. He took the spade from her, set his boot on the blade's top edge, and sank it effortlessly into the earth. "Why not let the servants do this for you?"

"I like doing it. What kind of project?"

"A monastery."

Main Body Text
Double Space
0.5" indentations

m. He couldn't be serious.

e," he said. "A priory, she calls it."

Example of correct manuscript format

→ Kyle/The Queen's Captive/84

r small or covered with honey and feathers. Why involve yourself in such a thing? Especially with Frances Grenville."

"It's hardly involvement." He flung a spade full of stony dirt toward the raspberry canes trained on a wooden lattice, and frowned as pebbles clattered against the latticework. "What did you plant last year, stones?"

"Roses like stony soil. How much are you donating?"

He rested his hand on the top of the spade handle and gave her an indulgent smile. "Don't worry, it's just a token. It'll be mostly her money."

"Then why involve you at all?"

With a shove of his boot, he dug the spade in again. "She wants someone to help her make decisions."

"There's her brother."

"You're right. The fact is, she has another motive. Her idea is to mend the rift between us, the two families."

Honor took back the spade and hacked the soil with a vigor that took the place of the retort on the tip of her tongue: *a little late for that.* "She could have just invited me to supper," she muttered as she dug.

Adam shrugged. "I think she's a rather lonely old lady."

Honor had to laugh. "She wouldn't appreciate you calling her old. She's of an age with her friend the Queen. Forty, perhaps."

He seemed mystified at the correction. "Exactly."

Example of correct manuscript format

There is no need to insert a copyright symbol anywhere on your manuscript, nor do you need to register your work with a copyright office. Copyright is instantaneous the moment you create a piece of writing, and the legal fact is that you own all rights in your work. If a publisher accepts your book, you negotiate a contract by which you assign certain publishing rights to the publisher—the contract will stipulate such things as territory (for example, world or North America), publication format (hardcover, paperback, e-book), duration, etc.—and the publisher will then copyright the book in your name. Some writers, anxious about protecting their ownership in the work, will mail themselves a copy of their own manuscript using registered mail; upon receiving the package they leave it unopened, and its postmark date is proof of their ownership. Do this if you want, but it's not necessary. One last word about copyright: titles cannot be copyrighted, and ideas cannot be copyrighted.

Finding an Agent

You now have a perfectly formatted, pristine, professional looking manuscript. What do you do to get it onto a publisher's desk? What you *don't* do is send it off to a publisher. No major publishing house, and few small ones either, will look at an unsolicited manuscript. An unsolicited manuscript is one that they have not requested. (The process of getting a publisher or agent to request your manuscript is addressed later in this chapter.)

If a writer does send their manuscript, unsolicited, to the offices of a publisher, this is what will likely happen. It goes into what the industry calls the "slush pile." Every now and then, an editor's assistant will be assigned to read the manuscripts in the slush pile. Rarely is there anything there that's worth publishing. Perhaps it's because any writer who hasn't even made the effort to find out how to submit a manuscript in the proper way has likely not made the effort to write a good book either.

Still, let's say this assistant finds a manuscript that she thinks is pretty good. Now, she faces a challenge. She must interest an acquisition editor in it—this is an editor who has the authority within the publishing company to make an offer for the book. But all the company's acquisition editors (large publishers employ many) are already overworked managing a score of projects, including reading manuscripts they *did* solicit. They're dealing all day with authors' deadlines, production schedules, agents' calls and emails, and sales conference preparation, as well as doing their main job of editing manuscripts. The result is that they are unlikely to have the time or inclination to even look at something an assistant brings them.

The accepted way to approach any publisher is with a query letter. (The term "letter" persists, even though most queries are now done by email. Here, and elsewhere, you will see "query letter" and "query" used interchangeably.) The query letter is addressed to a specific individual, and its purpose is to ask that person to read your manuscript. Your query can be sent by two possible routes. The first is to an acquisition editor within a publishing company. That is, you make a direct request that they consider reading your manuscript and publishing it. The second is to a literary agent. That is, you request that they consider reading your manuscript and representing you in offering your book to publishers. (Note: the references here to "editor" mean an *employee* in the editorial department of a publishing house. This should not be confused with a *freelance* editor who may work with a writer to prepare the writer's manuscript for submission to an agent or an acquisition editor.)

It's generally agreed that the second path—representation by an agent—offers your best chance for breaking in, because publishers are far more likely to want to read your manuscript if it comes to them through an agent. The publisher knows that the agent has already weeded out unpromising manuscripts. In representing you, the agent gives a stamp of approval that a publisher can usually rely on.

Agents are book-marketing experts. They have contacts throughout the publishing world. They deal with editors at publishing houses every day, discussing authors, negotiating contracts, keeping abreast of trends. They attend book fairs and book conferences and literary social events, constantly networking with editors, getting a feel for each editor's personal taste in books. All of this helps them sense which editor at which house might be most interested in acquiring any given book.

You pay an agent nothing up front; only once they have "sold" your book to a publisher do you pay their commission. It's something like working with a real-estate agent, who receives their sales commission only when they sell your house. The difference is that, unlike a real-estate agent whose role ends with the one-time sale of your house, a literary agent collects commission on your book sales as long as the book continues to garner royalties. A literary agent's standard commission is fifteen percent of what you earn from sales of your books, and twenty percent of foreign sales. For this commission you can expect an agent to do four main things for you:

- Place your book with a publisher
- Negotiate the publishing contract on your behalf
- Negotiate contracts for foreign rights, audiobook rights, and possibly film rights etc., on your behalf
- Offer some editing assistance at no charge. Some agents are excellent editors and will work with a writer through draft after draft of revisions, while others do not involve themselves to such a large extent.

Most agents, like publishers, will not look at an unsolicited manuscript—that is, one they have not asked to see. So your job as an emerging writer is to pitch your book to agents to get them interested in it and wanting to read it. To do that, you send them a query letter. The query is the standard way to ask any agent to read your work. Agents post guidelines on their websites about how to query them. For example, some want a synopsis of the book sent along with the query, while others don't.

To find agents, look through agent lists. There are several sources, including:

- Agent Query at www.AgentQuery.com
- Literary Marketplace, available in reference libraries or online at www.literarymarketplace.com.
- The Association of Authors' Representatives at www.aar-online.org.
- The Writers Digest Books annual *Guide To Literary Agents*

Pore over all these agent lists for the information you need. For example, different agents handle different types of fiction. If one says in the listing that they don't want to see any fantasy, don't query them about your fantasy novel. Agents are just people; they have likes and dislikes. Often, you can get a sense of their tastes from information in the listings. You can also see what books they've sold to publishers in the last year. Look for agents who handle a lot of the genre you're writing. From the lists, pick thirty or so who sound like they are compatible with selling the type of book you've written. These are the ones you will query.

Here's a tip: Read the acknowledgements in recent novels published in your genre. Chances are the author has thanked their agent. If so, put that agent's name on your list.

Your novel must be finished before you query an agent. If they ask to read the manuscript, it's got to be ready to go out the door the next day. Non-fiction books are different; publishers often buy non-fiction based on the writer's book proposal. Not so with a novel; it must be finished.

The Query Letter

The query letter may be the most important piece of writing you will ever do. You get only one chance to interest an agent in your book. As former agent Nathan Bransford says, "A query is part business letter, part creative writing exercise, part introduction, part death-defying leap through a flaming hoop."

The query letter is a sales pitch, pure and simple. Its sole purpose is to intrigue a busy publishing industry professional enough to want to read your story. A successful query is one that gets the agent to ask you to send them your manuscript.

Agents and editors get dozens of queries every day. So, the bad news is that you have about ten seconds to get this busy person intrigued about your book. The good news is that most query letters are badly written and, therefore, instantly fail. You have an opportunity to make your query a winner.

10 Tips for Writing a Successful Query

1. Limit your query to one page. Even for an email, stick to the one-page rule. It's what publishing professionals expect (and they are so overburdened with reading, they don't take kindly to long letters). You can say everything that's necessary on one page, single-spaced.

2. Structure your query in five brief sections: introduction, basics, hook, mini-synopsis, bio.

3. Introduction. This is your chance to connect with this agent or editor on a human level. If you enjoyed a talk they gave at a conference, say so. If you love her blog, say so. If you're a fan of an author he represents or publishes, tell him that. Be real. Build rapport.

4. Give the basics: your book's title (in caps), its genre (e.g. mystery, romance, thriller, YA fantasy), and the word count rounded off to the nearest hundred. Publishing industry professionals determine book length by word count, not page count. Use the word count function on your computer. The rule of thumb is 250 words per double-spaced page.

5. Deliver a dynamic hook: one concise and intriguing sentence about the story. For example: "*The Kite Runner* is a tale of fathers and sons, of friendship and betrayal, that sweeps from Afghanistan in the final days of the monarchy to the atrocities of the present."

6. Write a mini-synopsis of your story in two or three short paragraphs. This is hellishly hard, like trying to enclose an

ocean inside a bottle. My advice is don't try to cram in the entire plot; it will make you crazy. Stick to the central character and the story's central conflict. Don't get sidetracked into subplots or theme. Read the back covers of books in your genre and note how the publisher has described the story's protagonist and conflict in a single, engaging paragraph. That's the effect to aim for.

7. Include in #6 one or two comparables. A comparable is a successful book you mention to explain the intended target audience of your book. Agents and acquisition editors need to know where your book fits into the market. A good way to phrase this is that your book "would appeal to fans of [author]'" or is "in the vein of [book]." Keep it recent; publishers aren't interested in what sold three decades ago. And keep it rational; no inflated boasts about how your book will be a bestseller.

8. The last section is your bio. Keep it short—one brief paragraph—and preferably related to writing. For example, mention anything you've had published, such as a short story, or any writing contest you've won. If you've had nothing published, stick to info about yourself that you feel might be of interest.

9. Finally, close your query by saying the full manuscript is available, and make your "ask"—ask if you may send it to them for their consideration. And thank them for their time.

10. Send as many queries as you like. The rule about not sending "multiple submissions" applies only to a manuscript, and only once it's been requested. For queries, you may broadcast them.

Usually, you will hear back from a query within about two weeks. Be prepared: most agents will say they're not interested. Perhaps they aren't taking more clients at that time, or perhaps they don't handle your type of book. If an agent *is* interested, they will ask you to send a "partial"—the publishing industry's term for a partial manuscript —which is often the first chapter or the first fifty pages. If they like the partial and want to read the whole manuscript they'll get back to you and request a "full."

Once you've sent a full to an agent, give them time to read it. They have many other clients they represent, and many other manuscripts to read. A two-month wait is common. Three months isn't unreasonable. After three months, it's fine to reach out to them with a follow-up note.

Pitching in Person

Writers' conferences commonly offer pitch sessions, a chance for writers to pitch their story to an agent or an acquisition editor face-to-face. It's an excellent opportunity for any emerging writer, because you are your book's best advocate; you know your characters intimately. And pitching to an agent in person carries a "live" vitality that a query email lacks. Still, if you've never pitched before, you may be a little nervous, especially since you'll likely be given just five minutes with the agent, talking across a table. So, to help you, here are my five tips for how to stay on track and get the best results.

1. Be Prepared.

Practice is the key. Write your pitch, and rewrite it. Then rehearse it until you can deliver it smoothly.

2. Keep It Short.

If your session is five minutes long, keep your pitch to under two minutes: ninety seconds is about right. That leaves a few minutes for the agent to ask you questions. If she's intrigued by your story she'll ask you to send a partial, or perhaps even a full. If there's time, ask a question yourself. For example, ask about the average publication process.

3. Keep It Focused.

Be concise. Don't ramble. Don't veer off into your book's theme or "message." Keep your pitch character-driven; that is, stick to your main character's goal and what she or he wants, and the story's central conflict. Also, you don't have to give away the ending. Remember, the pitch is to whet the agent's interest, to make them want to hear more.

4. Be Professional.

A pitch session is a business meeting, so present yourself professionally. You're not there to chat, or discuss writing craft; you're there to interest the agent in your story enough to request a look at it. The more prepared and professional you are, the more you convey your commitment. Agents appreciate that because they're committed to their work too.

5. Build on the Experience.

The pitch session is your chance to make an important one-on-one connection with an agent. It may land you representation, and even, eventually, a publishing deal. But even if that doesn't happen you'll gain invaluable experience in pitching, which is a crucial part of our business. You'll learn a lot about what agents look for, about the market, and your book's possible place in it. If you don't try, you'll never know.

It may take you a while to break into the business, but don't give up. Most successful authors experienced plenty of rejections before they broke in. Like you, they learned, and kept at it until they had crafted a story so good, it captured the heart and commitment of an agent and then of a publisher. They persevered until they had created a page-turner.

So keep learning, and keep persevering. Grow as a writer. Dare to succeed.

CHAPTER 10

TIPS FROM A FIRST
DRAFT SURVIVOR

I'm a veteran. In the great war of Being an Author, I have been in the trenches, and survived. I've had eleven novels published, and in over twenty years of writing I've faced every challenge you're facing now. So I know what you're going through. I've been there. I'm an old soldier.

Writing a novel takes many months of hard slogging. To produce a book that is both compelling and marketable, writers need all the help we can get. So, let me share with you some of the ways I get through that long slog to finish a novel. Every writer works differently, of course, but this is how it's been for me. And I hope that hearing some of my experiences will help you as you labor through your first draft and the drafts that follow.

Here are my seven tips for survival.

Tip #1. Get Dressed.

When I sit down to write at home, I don't do it in a ratty old dressing gown and slippers. I get dressed as if I'm going out into the world to work. I take a shower, put on clean clothes, brush my hair, and go to meet my characters.

There's a story about Florenz Ziegfeld and his famous "Ziegfeld Follies" of the 1920s. These were lavish Broadway shows filled with beautiful girls in stunning, although scanty, costumes. One day, Ziegfeld was watching a rehearsal, and he thought the girls seemed to have lost their zip. They didn't look sexy. He wondered if it was because they didn't *feel* sexy. So he told the stage manager to order the finest pure silk underwear for every girl. The stage manager was a little dismayed. "Why go to all that expense?" he said. "The audience won't know the girls are wearing silk underwear." Ziegfeld replied, "The girls will know."

Now, you may or may not want to wear silk underwear when you write. The point is: it's all in the head. That's why I get dressed to go to work.

Tip #2: Rely on Routine.

You write because you're creative. So why is creating so difficult? I believe it's the tyranny of expectations. You sit down in front of that blank screen, and you have to produce. I don't know a writer anywhere who isn't somewhat cowed by that pressure.

Part of the pressure is because you're all alone. Writing is such a solitary endeavor. We writers work without benefit of the collaborative vigor that energizes actors, musicians, and dancers.

For me, the good news was finding out that I wasn't really alone. I had two steadfast old friends, Routine and Ritual, and they have supported me through good times and bad.

Here's a paradox: to allow your imagination to roam free, maintain order in your life. I've found that ritual and routine liberate my creativity. The reason is that I need to restrict the distractions around me. I stick to the routines and rituals that maintain calmness in my world. I need only three things to write: quiet, heat, and a continuous supply of tea. Three simple things, but without them I cannot work. Especially quiet. Even hearing a radio down the hall distracts me. I don't do mental multi-tasking.

My routine goes like this. My workday starts around eight a.m., so I'm at my desk then, mug of tea beside me, phone ready to be ignored, invitations to lunch already declined. First, I spend a couple of hours on business, replying to emails, doing promotion such as returning interview answers or interacting on social media. Then, at around ten, I write.

My writing routine always is to start with rewriting the material I wrote the day before. I love re-writing and fixing, so I have to cut myself off at noon; if I didn't, I'd go on all day. At noon I grab a sandwich and often bring it back to my desk. Then I write until about four, working on the new patch of material. When I'm writing a novel's first draft, I aim to create five pages a day, but I'm lucky if I accomplish that. It's usually three to four pages. At about four o'clock I go for an hour's walk, summer or winter. There are interesting studies showing that walking is very conducive to creativity. I've definitely found that.

So, that's my routine, and it rarely varies. It gives me a comforting continuity during the brain-teasing, hair-pulling frustrations of plotting and writing a novel.

As for rituals, one of mine is to have the same thing for lunch for days on end. A grilled cheese sandwich or a bowl of minestrone or a bean burrito. (Yup, I'm a vegetarian.) Whatever it is, I'll have it day after day. I like the sameness. Often, when the book changes gears that's when I change my sandwich.

For you, the rituals and routines may be very different. The point is, whichever ones work for you, go with them. Take comfort from them. Rely on them.

Tip #3. Don't Beat Yourself Up.

You may have read advice in books about writing that say you should write every day, even if it's just for an hour. I used to say this too to new writers, but I've found that it inflicts an unnecessary burden. I don't want you to beat yourself up for having not written anything for days on end. Guilt is not productive. After all, most people who are working on a novel are also holding down a full-time job, or taking care of young children all day. It can be hard to find the *time* to write. So no, you really don't have to write every day.

What you *do* have to do is that when you write, make it count. No dabbling. Make that writing period sacrosanct. Before I wrote full time my career was acting, and I did a lot of musical theater. I studied singing with a wonderful coach who'd had starring roles with the New York City Opera. She had an expression about her daily home practicing that I liked. She said that whenever she practiced, she stepped into an imaginary "circle of quality." Inside that circle, she did only her best work.

I try to do the same with my writing. And I recommend it to you. Every time you sit down to write, imagine a circle of quality around your desk and step into that circle. It doesn't mean you're going to write brilliantly. That's an objective judgment, and you can't even be thinking about that. It means you're going to write *seriously*. No half-hearted dabbling. Step into that circle of quality every time, and do your best work.

TIP #4: READ THE GOOD AND THE BAD.

I try to read great books, of course, but I read bad books too, and I'd like to say a word in praise of bad books. I've learned a lot from them. With a really good book, it's often hard to see how the author did it. Their work is so seamless, it becomes invisible. Also, the story is so compelling I get drawn into it like any reader and I stop examining the structure, stop studying it. I've re-read Ian McEwan's novel *Atonement* a couple of times to study it, and each time I had to force myself to resist getting so involved again with the characters, caring so deeply about their dilemmas, that I'd forget to study it.

But with a poorly written book, one that doesn't get you caring, one that's plain boring, it's easy to stay detached. More important, it's often easy to see *why* the book doesn't work, be it a fault of craft like a passive, unempathetic protagonist, a weak antagonist, no clear conflict, too few dramatic turning points, or a flat unsatisfying climax—faults not present in good novels. So I recommend studying both kinds, the good and the bad. Don't read as a *consumer* of art but as a *producer* of art. Keep reading, and keep learning.

By the way, new writers sometimes look at the output of star writers and say, "I can write better than that." Perhaps they can.

But, if you look at the first novels that made those writers stars, almost invariably they are compelling books. Later, because of these writers' enormous success, they're under pressure to turn out a book a year, so their subsequent books can sometimes suffer. Because they're stars, it doesn't matter; their publishers will gladly print whatever they write, knowing it will sell. Not so in the case of the emerging writer. To get published, a new writer has to write a really compelling book, just as the stars did.

Tip #5. Take Time to Think.

I spend a lot of time daydreaming. I'm at work. I'm thinking of how to bring in my inciting incident earlier. Or I'm pondering how to turn a scene by introducing a reversal. Or I'm trying to find the most powerful way to build the climax so that my protagonist and antagonist come into direct confrontation. Don't let anybody tell you you're wasting your time when you're staring out a window for half an hour. You're at work. You're trying to figure out all the elements of craft that I just mentioned, and many more.

Also, don't censor your thinking. Explore everything that comes to you. Sift, reflect, prioritize your thoughts. But don't censor.

Tip #6. Don't Expect Your Family to Understand.

I can almost see you nodding. You know this one already.

I have two brothers. My late mother would never have dreamed of phoning them at their offices to chat, because they're busy with work, but she'd phone me because, in her mind, I wasn't working, just writing. Be aware that some of your friends and family won't understand what you're wrestling with as you hone your craft. They won't understand the concentration and time it requires.

However, if you take your work seriously it has a subtle effect on the people around you—your partner, your children, your friends. They'll catch on about your commitment. They'll start to respect it. They may occasionally grumble, but they'll respect it.

Here's the other thing. While you should not expect your family to understand what you do, there are people who *do* understand. Other writers. They, and they alone, know what you're going through. The frustrations. The highs. The setbacks. The lows. The sheer joy in the work despite the lows. The obsession. Rely on other writers in your life. They get it.

Tip #7. Keep Your Expectations Low and Your Standards High.

There are two guiding principles I've developed for survival at my writing desk. They've helped me stay the course in creating all my books, and I hope they'll sustain you too, and get you through your rough patches.

Years ago, when my writing wasn't going well, I'd get discouraged and dread going to my desk. It was what I now call the tyranny of expectations—sitting down in front of that blank screen and feeling the awful pressure that I had to produce something good. Every morning I'd sit in the kitchen with my mug of tea for as long as possible, reading the newspaper from front to back, dragging it out to avoid walking down the hall to my office, because I felt *I just can't do it. I can't go in there and write something good.*

Then one day I got so frustrated I actually said out loud, "Well, damn it, I'll go in and write something bad."

It was instant liberation. The pressure evaporated. Because I knew I could write something bad. So I went into my office and sat down ... and I *did* write something bad. Hallelujah!

Which brings me to guiding principle #1: Give yourself permission to write something bad.

Because here's guiding principle #2: Everything can be fixed.

It's true. You can rewrite and fix something that's bad, but you cannot fix something that doesn't exist. All my novels started out as unfocused, sprawling outlines. But I fixed them. They turned out to be very good books. So there it is: give yourself permission to write something bad, secure in the knowledge that everything can be fixed.

Remember—it's a process. Embrace the work.

Your Bookshelf:
Suggested Resources

Forster, E.M. ASPECTS OF THE NOVEL. Harcourt Brace
   Jovanovich, 1927
Though old and hard to find, this book is a gem.

Gardner, John. THE ART OF FICTION. Vintage Books,
   reissue edition 1991
A classic.

George, Elizabeth. WRITE AWAY. Harper Perennial; reprint
   edition 2005
*George delivers a down-to-earth guide on craft, augmented by her
personal insights on the creative process. If I had to recommend just
one book on writing, this would be it.*

King, Stephen. ON WRITING: A MEMOIR OF THE CRAFT.
   Pocketbooks, 2002
*An entertaining master class on craft from one of the bestselling
authors of all time.*

Lukeman, Noah. THE FIRST FIVE PAGES: A WRITER'S
GUIDE TO STAYING OUT OF THE REJECTION
PILE. Fireside/Simon & Schuster, 2000
*Literary agent Lukeman gives good advice. The first chapter outlines
the basics of manuscript formatting, essential for submitting fiction
to a publisher or agent.*

McKee, Robert. STORY. ReganBooks, HarperCollins, 1997
*Written for screenwriters, but invaluable for all writers. McKee's
seminars on "Story" regularly sell out around the world.*

Vogler, Christopher. THE WRITER'S JOURNEY: MYTHIC
STRUCTURE FOR WRITERS. Michael Wiese
Productions, 3rd Edition 2007
*A "light bulb" book for every writer. Vogler explains how to
understand and use the enduring principles of myth to create pow-
erful stories.*

Zuckerman, Albert. WRITING THE BLOCKBUSTER
NOVEL. Forge Books, revised edition 2016.
*Legendary New York literary agent Al Zuckerman has been "mid-
wife" to dozens of bestsellers. Study the sage precepts in his superb book.*

Invaluable Basic Books:

Strunk, William and White, E.B. THE ELEMENTS OF
  STYLE. Longman, 1999; fourth edition.
A timeless handbook, first published in 1959.

Truss, Lynne. EATS, SHOOTS & LEAVES. Gotham; reprint
  edition 2006
The witty and wise bestseller about punctuation.

Zinsser, William. ON WRITING WELL. Harper Perennial;
  30th Anniversary Edition 2006
*Zinsser's classic guide to writing non-fiction is inspiration for fiction
writers too.*

# # #

Printed in Great Britain
by Amazon